# BY CHARLES REZNIKOFF

# POEMS 1918-1936 VOLUME I OF THE COMPLETE POEMS OF CHARLES REZNIKOFF

*EDITED BY*
*SEAMUS COONEY*

*BLACK SPARROW PRESS • SANTA BARBARA • 1978*

The publisher and the editor would like to thank the National Endowment for the Arts for a grant which has helped in the continuation of this project.

LIBRARY OF CONGRESS CATALOGING IN PUBLICATION DATA

Reznikoff, Charles, 1894-1976
    Poems, 1918-1936.

    Includes index.
PS3535.E98A17   1976            811'.5'2            75-44423
ISBN 0-87685-261-4 pbk.
ISBN 0-87685-262-2

Second Printing

# EDITOR'S NOTE

My purpose has been to make authoritative texts readily available. The author's latest revisions have been followed in every case, with one qualification. When Mr. Reznikoff made a selection of his poems for the 1962 New Directions volume, *By the Waters of Manhattan*, he adopted for the early poems which he chose the typographical style he began using somewhat later: that is, he dropped the convention of capital letters at the beginning of each verse line (first done in *Jerusalem the Golden* in 1934), assigned numbers to all the poems, and used arabic in preference to roman numerals. I have applied these practices consistently throughout this book.

For the reader interested in the process of poetic growth and revision, the Appendix gives full details (I hope unobtrusively), together with the texts of poems the author omitted from later printings.

Volume Two of the *Collected Poems*, covering the years from 1937 to the present, will follow shortly, and will be succeeded by the first installment of Reznikoff's monumental poem *Testimony: The United States*, which in itself will run several volumes. Finally, a volume of the *Collected Plays* is planned. In due course we hope eventually to get the bulk of Charles Reznikoff's work back in print.

Seamus Cooney
Western Michigan University
Kalamazoo

# TABLE OF CONTENTS

# Poems 1918-1936

# I
# Rhythms
# 1918

*Rhythms*, Reznikoff's first book, was published by the author in Brooklyn, New York, in 1918. It contained twenty-three unnumbered poems. When he reprinted the group in *Poems* (1920), Reznikoff rearranged the order, dropped five poems, and revised thirteen others. He again revised and rearranged the group for the 1927 book, *Five Groups of Verse,* restoring one of the omitted poems. This third version is the one reproduced here. For details of the re-orderings and revisions and for the omitted poems see the Appendix.

The stars are hidden,
the lights are out;
the tall black houses
are ranked about.

I beat my fists
on the stout doors,
no answering steps
come down the floors.

I have walked until
I am faint and numb;
from one dark street
to another I come.

The comforting
winds are still.

This is a chaos
through which I stumble,
till I reach the void
and down I tumble.

The stars will then
be out forever;
the fists unclenched,
the feet walk never,

and all I say
blown by the wind
away.

The dead are walking silently.

I sank them six feet underground,
the dead are walking and no sound.

I raised on each a brown hill,
the dead are walking slow and still.

So one day, tired of the sky and host of stars,
I'll thrust the tinsel by.

I step into the fishy pool
as if into a cool
vault.
I, too, become
cold-blooded, dumb.

The dead man lies in the street.
They spread a sack over his bleeding head.
It drizzles. Gutter and walks are black.

His wife now at her window,
the supper done, the table set,
waits for his coming out of the wet.

They dug her grave so deep
no voice can creep to her.

She can feel no stir
of joy when her girl sings,

and quietly she lies
when her girl cries.

On Brooklyn Bridge I saw a man drop dead.
It meant no more than if he were a sparrow.

Above us rose Manhattan;
below, the river spread to meet sea and sky.

I met in a merchant's place
Diana:
lithe body and flowerlike face.

Through the woods I had looked for her
and beside the waves.

The shopgirls leave their work
quietly.

Machines are still, tables and chairs
darken.

The silent rounds of mice and roaches begin.

Hair and faces glossy with sweat in August
at night through narrow streets glaring with lights
people as if in funeral processions;
on stoops weeds in stagnant pools,
at windows waiting for a wind that never comes.
Only, a lidless eye, the sun again.

No one else in the street but a wind blowing,
store-lamps dimmed behind frosted panes,
stars, like the sun broken and scattered in bits.

I walked through the lonely marsh
among the white birches.

Above the birches rose
three crows,
croaking, croaking.

The trumpets blare war
and the streets are filled with the echoes.

Wringing, wringing his pierced hands,
he walks in a wood where once a flood
washed the ground into loose white sand;
and the trees stand each a twisted cross,
smooth and white with loss of leaves and bark,
together like warped yards and masts
of a fleet at anchor centuries.
No blasts come to the hollow of these dead;
long since the water has gone from the stony bed.
No fields and streets for him, his pathway runs
among these skeletons, through these white sands,
wringing, wringing his pierced hands.

## Romance

The troopers are riding, are riding by,
the troopers are riding to kill and die
that a clean flag may cleanly fly.

They touch the dust in their homes no more,
they are clean of the dirt of shop and store,
and they ride out clean to war.

How shall we mourn you who are killed and wasted,
sure that you would not die with your work unended,
as if the iron scythe in the grass stops for a flower?

Her kindliness is like the sun
toward dusk shining through a tree.

Her understanding is like the sun,
shining through mist on a width of sea.

16

The fingers of your thoughts
are moulding your face
ceaselessly.

The wavelets of your thoughts
are washing your face
beautiful.

17

When you sang moving your body proudly
before me wondering who you were
suddenly I remembered, Messalina.

18

The sea's white teeth
nibble the cliff;
the cliff is a man,
unafraid.

She eats his strength
little by little,
his might will be lost
in her depths.

19

My work done, I lean on the window-sill,
watching the dripping trees.
The rain is over, the wet pavement shines.
From the bare twigs
rows of drops like shining buds are hanging.

# II
# Rhythms II
# 1919

*Rhythms II* was published by the author in Brooklyn, New York, in 1919. It too contained twenty-three unnumbered poems. For *Poems* (1920) Reznikoff rearranged the sequence, combined two poems into one, revised ten others, and added two new ones. For *Five Groups of Verse* (1927), he again rearranged the order, revised two poems, and dropped two. As a final revision, in the 1962 selection one poem had its title deleted. The present text follows the 1927 version with that one deletion. For details of the reorderings and revisions and for the omitted poems see the Appendix.

## 1

I have not even been in the fields,
nor lain my fill in the soft foam,
and here you come blowing, cold wind.

## 2

### Vaudeville

I leave the theatre,
keeping step, keeping step to the music.
It sticks to my feet,
stepped into dung.

Night falls
in still flakes.

## 3

I knocked. A strange voice answered.
So they, too, have moved away.

We had walked up and down the block many times
until alone.

I wonder where they have moved to.

## 4

I look across the housetops,
through the leaves in a black pattern:
where are you hidden, moon?

Surely I saw her,
broad-bosomed and golden,
coming toward us.

## 5

The winter afternoon darkens.
The shoemaker bends close to the shoe,
his hammer raps faster.

An old woman waits,
rubbing the cold from her hands.

6

Stubborn flies buzzing
in the morning when she wakes.

The flat roofs, higher, lower,
chimneys, water-tanks, cornices.

7

## Scrubwoman

One shoulder lower,
with unsure step like a bear erect,
the smell of the wet black rags that she cleans with about her.

Scratching with four stiff fingers her half-bald head,
smiling.

8

In the shop, she, her mother, and grandmother,
thinking at times of women at windows in still streets,
or women reading, a glow on resting hands.

9

## The Idiot

With green stagnant eyes,
arms and legs
loose ends of string in a wind,

keep smiling at your father.

10

On the kitchen shelf the dusty medicine bottles;
she in her room heaped under a sheet,
and men and women coming in with clumsy steps.

She who worked patiently,
her children grown,
lies in her grave patiently.

Beggars about the streets
pray to God between set teeth.

Up by star and star
until the outer frozen blackness,

down the earth between stones
until black rocks in ledge on ledge.

## The Park in Winter

It rains.
The elms curve into clouds of twigs.
The lawns are empty.

Dark early and only the river shines
like grey ice, the ships moored fast.

## Epidemic

Streamers of crepe idling before doors.

Shadows, mice whisk over the unswept floor,
tumble through rustling papers.

Squeeze into desk drawers,
biting the paper into yellowed flakes
and leaving crumbs of filth.

## 17

The sandwiches are elaborate affairs:
toast, bacon, toast, chicken, toast.

We sip our coffee watching the rouged women
walk quickly to their seats, unsmiling, contemptuous.

## 18

The imperious dawn comes
to the clink of milk bottles
and round-shouldered sparrows twittering.

## 19

We heard no step in the hall.
She came
sudden as a rainbow.

## 20

A white curtain turning in an open window.

A swan, dipping a white neck in the trees' shadow,
hardly beating the water with golden feet.

Sorrow before her
was gone like noise from a street,
snow falling.

## 21

The horses keep tossing their heads and stamp the hollow
    flooring,
wheel knocks into wheel
as the ferry glides out into a damp wind.

The coal-truck horses, three abreast, ponderously,
sides and rumps shaking.

With blown manes and tails
the horses fling themselves along lifting their riders.

24

The thin horses step beside the lawns in the park,
the small hoofs newly oiled,
heads high, their red nostrils taking the air.

22

**Twilight**

No stars
in the blue curve
of the heavens,
no wind.

Far off,
a white horse
in the green gloom
of the meadow.

# III
# Poems
# 1920

*Poems* was published by Samuel Roth at the New York Poetry Book Shop, 49 West Eighth Street, in 1920. It contained unnumbered revised versions of the contents of the two earlier books and thirty-nine new poems, thirty-two unnumbered and the others in two groups with the collective titles "Nightmares" and "Four of Us." For *Five Groups of Verse* Reznikoff dropped about a fifth of the new poems and revised most of the others. The present text follows that revision, except for one poem further revised for the 1962 selection. For details of the reordering and revisions and for the omitted poems see the Appendix.

### 1

The sun was low over the blue morning water;
the waves of the bay were silent on the smooth beach,
where in the night the silver fish had died gasping.

### 2

Old men and boys search the wet garbage with fingers
and slip pieces in bags.

This fat old man has found the hard end of a bread
and bites it.

### 3

The girls outshout the machines
and she strains for their words, blushing.

Soon she, too, will speak
their speech glibly.

### 4

The pedlar who goes from shop to shop,
has seated himself on the stairs in the dim hallway,
and the basket of apples upon his knees, breathes the odor.

### 5

Her work was to count linings—
the day's seconds in dozens.

### 6

They have built red factories along Lake Michigan,
and the purple refuse coils like congers in the green depths.

### 7

The house-wreckers have left the door and a staircase,
now leading to the empty room of night.

## Ghetto Funeral

Followed by his lodge, shabby men stumbling over the
    cobblestones,
and his children, faces red and ugly with tears, eyes and
    eyelids red,
in the black coffin in the black hearse the old man.

No longer secretly grieving
that his children are not strong enough to go the way he
    wanted to go
and was not strong enough.

9

Showing a torn sleeve, with stiff and shaking fingers the old
    man
pulls off a bit of the baked apple, shiny with sugar,
eating with reverence food, the great comforter.

10

Sleepless, breathing the black air, he heard footsteps along the
    street,
and click—the street-lamp was out;
darkness jumped like a black cat upon his chest.

Dawn: the window became grey,
the bed-clothes were lit up and his sleeping wife's head,
as if the darkness had melted into that heap of loose hair.

Soon her eyes would open, disks of light blue, strange in a
    Jewess.
He would turn away; the eyes would look curiously, the way
    they had been looking for months,
how are you getting on? still not doing well?
And her left hand would raise itself slowly and pull on the
    lobe of her left ear;
and her eyes shine with a slight pity, the way a woman looks
    at a mouse in a trap.

No longer the calm look with which she had greeted him,
when he was chief clerk in a store in that Russian town
which he now carried about like picture postal-cards in a
        pocket,
the town where he had shone in the light of the big store.

Day: the noise of splashing water, his children in underwear
        thudding about with bare feet,
pulling on clothes in a hurry and bending over to lace shoes.
Soon the door would close, again and again, all would be
        gone,
the elder to shops, the younger ones to school.
For these he had come to America that they might study and
        the boys be free from army service,
to lift and spread them as he had been doing, boughs of
        himself, the trunk.
Now the elder were going to work and could study only at
        night,
snipping bits for years, perhaps ten or more, to make their
        patched learning,
and pooling wages to buy food and lodging for the younger
        children, his wife, and himself.
He could only bring them food from the kitchen,
or run downstairs to the grocer's for pickles or a bottle of
        ketchup—
to make life tastier,
to try to stick hairs in the hide of life and make it a fur to wrap ⌉
        them snug.                                                 ⌋
Forty years in a store where business was done leisurely over
        glasses of tea,
and now to walk the streets and meet men hasty and abrupt,
between tenements and their barrels heaped with ashes and
        garbage.
Younger relatives now excused themselves after a few words
and hurried into the noise of their shops to some matter of
        their own.
If only his business were not a flower-pot into which he had
        spilled his savings
day by day carefully and had spilled loans—
and nothing came up from the black earth.

The day was the first warm day of spring.
The sunlight through the windowpanes fell in large living

oblongs on the floor.
He opened a window; the air blew in, warm and fragrant.
The sunlight fell on his shoes, cracked and gaping, his faded
    trousers, the bottoms frayed.

In winter, when rain drummed sullen marches on pavement
    and windowpanes,
or the streets were heaped with snow turning black,
his own music was sung and his despair imaged.
Now he was forgotten—easily, like the thought of somebody
    else's sorrow.
The yards and fire-escapes were glinting with sunlight, and the
    tall fences,
dirtied by rain, their rows of nails on top bleeding rust.

Women were opening windows and shaking out clothes,
his own wife had gone to the grocer's or butcher's, his children
    were at work or school;
only he was useless, like an old pot left in the kitchen for a
    while.

He pulled down the window-blind and laid himself near the
    stove.
He folded his coat under his head, over the floor's hardness.
The pour of gas sickened him, he was half-minded to pull the
    rubber tube out of his mouth;
but he felt dizzy, too weak to move.

11

She sat by the window opening into the airshaft,
and looked across the parapet
at the new moon.

She would have taken the hairpins out of her carefully coiled
    hair,
and thrown herself on the bed in tears;
but he was coming and her mouth had to be pinned into a smile.
If he would have her, she would marry whatever he was.

A knock. She lit the gas and opened her door.
Her aunt and the man—skin loose under his eyes, the face
    slashed with wrinkles.
"Come in," she said as gently as she could and smiled.

## 12

The house was pitch-dark.
He entered his room. Books and papers were heaped over the
     floor.
He stuck a candle in a corner, and on his knees began to go
     through the papers.
He must finish that night: the next day the others would move
     in.

Yes, here was the bold handwriting, the bundle of letters tied
     together.
He took these into the kitchen. He did not need a light:
he ought to know the way, had walked it so often.

He crammed all into the stove and lit a match.
The fire ran over the surface and died out.
He tore the letters into bits and lit match after match,
until nothing was left but brown pieces with black, crumbled
     edges.

As the papers twisted and opened, tormented by fire,
*Darling* had stood out in the writing against the flame
for a moment before the ink was grey on black ash that fell
     apart.

Here was the bedroom where she had been sick.
Her teeth fell out; before the end her nose rotted off.

He uncovered a bunch of dried flowers and white gauze—
her bridal veil and bouquet left in the rubbish.
He went back to the kitchen stove. The gauze flew up in a
     great flame, but the flowers remained—blackened stalks.
Now he was through. He closed door after door softly behind
     him.

## 13

From where she lay she could see the snow crossing the
     darkness slowly,
thick about the arc-lights like moths in summer.

She could just move her head. She had been lying so for
     months.

Her son was growing tall and broad-shouldered, his face
    becoming like that of her father,
dead now for years.

She lay under the bed-clothes as if she, too, were covered with
    snow,
calm, facing the blackness of night,
through which the snow fell in the crowded movement of stars.

Dead, nailed in a box, her son was being sent to her,
through fields and cities cold and white with snow.

## 14

The twigs tinge the winter sky
brown.

## 15

A slender tree, alone in the fields,
between the roofs of the town and the woods like a low hill.

In the open
the birds are faintly overheard.

## 16

### August

The city breaks in houses to the sea, uneasy with waves.
In the streets truck-horses, muscles sliding under the steaming
    hides,
pound the sparks flying about their hoofs.

## 17

In the streets children beneath tall houses at games greedily,
remembering clocks, the house-cats lapping time.

## 18

Kitten, pressed into a rude shape by cart wheels,
an end to your slinking away and trying to hide behind ash-cans.

The baby woke with curved, confiding fingers.
The gas had been turned down until it was only a yellow
    glimmer.
A rat walked slowly from under the washtub.

20

Ships dragged into the opaque green of the sea,
visible winds flinging houses apart—
and here the poplar roots lifting the pavement an inch.

21

Speaking and speaking again words like silver bubbles,
we walk at dusk through rain.

The sky has grown black with a tinge of red from the street-
    lamps;
triangular pools form in the square cracks of the pavement,
noisy with rain.

22

Suddenly we noticed that we were in darkness;
so we went into the house and lit the lamp.

The talk fell apart and bit by bit slid into a lake.
At last we rose and bidding each other good night went to our
    rooms.

In and about the house darkness lay, a black fog;
and each on his bed spoke to himself alone, making no sound.

23

Hour after hour in a rocking-chair on the porch,
hearing the wind in the shade trees.

At times a storm comes up and the dust is blown in long
    curves along the street,
over the carts driven slowly, drivers and horses nodding.

Years are thrown away as if I were immortal,
the nights spent in talking
shining words, sometimes, like fireflies in the darkness—
lighting and going out and after all no light.


24


I walked in a street, head high,
when a thug began beating a passer-by.

I gave no help with blow or cry,
but hurried on glad it wasn't I.


25


### Aphrodite Vrania

The ceaseless weaving of the uneven water.


26


### Moonlit Night

The trees' shadows lie in black pools on the lawns.


27


### April

The stiff lines of the twigs
blurred by buds.


28


I have watched trees and the moon and walked on—
she would be beauty to go wherever I go.


29


Still much to read, but too late.
I turn out the light.

The leaves of the tree are green beside the street-lamp;
the wind hardly blows and the tree makes no noise.

Tomorrow up early,
the crowded street-car, the factory.

30

A clerk tiptoeing the office floor
in a flurry of insignificant stuff;
or with samples from store to store
to speak politely to the gruff,
entering timidly the door,
trying to bow and smile it right
with smiles seen not true enough,
a young man who was so bright.

They spoke proudly and well,
fearing and revering none,
had no longing to buy and sell
or chatter with girls half the night;
what at last have these men done,
the young men who were so bright?

# IV
# Uriel Accosta: A Play and
# A Fourth Group of Verse
# 1921

*Uriel Accosta: A Play and A Fourth Group of Verse* was published by the author in New York in 1921. In addition to the verse play *Uriel Accosta*, almost half the volume consisted of new poems, twenty-four of them unnumbered and twenty-seven numbered under the collective title "Jews." For *Five Groups of Verse* (1927) Reznikoff rearranged the order (though leaving the "Jews" sequence largely intact), dropped two poems, and revised all but three of the others. The present text follows that of *Five Groups*. For details of the reordering and revisions and for the omitted poems see the Appendix.

## Sunday Walks in the Suburbs

On stones mossed with hot dust, no shade but the thin, useless
    shadows of roadside grasses;
into the wood's gloom, staring back at the blue flowers on
    stalks thin as threads.

The green slime—a thicket of young trees standing in brown
    water;
with knobs like muscles, a naked tree stretches up,
dead; and a dead duck, head sunk in the water as if diving.

The tide is out. Only a pool is left on the creek's stinking mud.
Someone has thrown a washboiler away.
On the bank a heap of cans;
rats, covered with rust, creep in and out.
The white edges of the clouds like veining in a stone.

2

Scared dogs looking backwards with patient eyes;
at windows stooping old women, wrapped in shawls;
old men, wrinkled as knuckles, on the stoops.

A bitch, backbone and ribs showing in the sinuous back,
sniffed for food, her swollen udder nearly rubbing along the
    pavement.

Once a toothless woman opened her door,
chewing a slice of bacon that hung from her mouth like a
    tongue.

This is where I walked night after night;
this is where I walked away many years.

3

## Beggar Woman

When I was four years old my mother led me to the park.
The spring sunshine was not too warm. The street was almost
    empty.

The witch in my fairy-book came walking along.
She stooped to fish some mouldy grapes out of the gutter.

4

## Railway Station at Cleveland

Under cloud on cloud the lake is black;
wheeling locomotives in the yard
pour their smoke into the crowded sky.

5

## Drizzle

Between factories the grease coils along the river.
Tugs drag their guts of smoke, like beetles stepped on.

6

Out of the hills the trees bulge;
the sky hangs in lumps of cloud.

7

All night the wind blew.
In the morning the deck-hands
were running around to warm up.
The boat rose and fell
on the little waves.
Now and then it hit
a chopping wave.
The wind blew the white caps of the water
into spray.
Far off the wild geese
were flying over the lake.

The lake was ridged with waves,
rolling between the shores.
The northern shore was cliff,
barren of houses or trees;
on the flat southern shore
towns spread out like patches.

There was no rest from the wind:
it blew steadily colder.
The deck-hands ran about,
beating their arms over their breasts.
The wild geese far away
were flying south in squads.

## 8

With broad bosom and hips, her head thrown back,
she parades, her high heels clacking,
having conquered troublesome youth and not yet afraid of age.

## 9

Head bowed beneath her black turban, she glances up at her
    daughter
who eyes in the mirror herself, yellow hair and beautiful face.

## 10

### A Tapestry

Isolde of the White Hands and her knights, holding their noses
    and laughing
at prisoners whose bellies soldiers open, pulling the guts into
    basins.

## 11

### Visiting

#### I

Almost midnight. "Good night." "Good night."
I close the heavy door behind me.
The black courtyard smells of water: it has been raining.
What were we talking about?

#### II

He leans back along the sofa. I talk. His fingers twitch at his
    bath-robe.
I talk. I turn my pockets inside out.
In his oblique eyes a polite disdain.

## 12

This noise in the subway will sound no louder than the wind
    in trees;
you, too, will be used to it. After a while you will forget to
    care
whether you ride in subways or on horses.

## 13

Sparrows scream at the dawn one note:
how should they learn melody
in the street's noises?

## 14

### Evening

The trees in the windless field like a herd asleep.

## 15

### Indian Summer

The men in the field are almost through stacking rows of pale
    yellow cornstalks.
On the lawn a girl is raking the leaves into a fire.

## 16

We children used to cross the orchard, the brown earth covered
    with little green apples,
into the field beyond;
the grass came up over our knees,
there were so many flowers we did not care to pick any—
daisies and yellow daisies, goldenrod and buttercups.
It was so hot the field smelt of cake baking.

## 17

After dinner, Sunday afternoons, we boys would walk slowly
to the lots between the streets and the marshes;
and seated under the pale blue sky would watch the ball game—

in a noisy, joyous crowd, lemonade men out in the fringe
    tinkling their bells beside their yellow carts.
As we walked back, the city stretched its rows of houses across
    the lots—
light after light, as the lamplighter went his way and women
    lit the gas in kitchens to make supper.

## 18

Swiftly the dawn became day. I went into the street.
Loudly and cheerfully the sparrows chirped.
The street-lamps were still lit, the sky pale and brightening.
Hidden in trees and on the roofs,
loudly and cheerfully the sparrows chirped.

## 19

He showed me the album. "But this?" I asked, surprised at
    such beauty.
I knew his sister, her face somewhat the picture's—coarsened.
"My mother before her marriage."
Coming in, I had met
her shrivelled face and round shoulders.
Now, after the day's work, his father at cards with friends
still outshouted the shop's wheels.
Afterwards, when I left, I had to go through their candy store
with its one showcase of candy,
in little heaps in little saucers, ever so many for a penny.
They kept no lights in the window. A single gas jet flared in
    the empty store.

## 20

It had long been dark, though still an hour before supper-time.
The boy stood at the window behind the curtain.
The street under the black sky was bluish white with snow.
Across the street, where the lot sloped to the pavement,
boys and girls were going down on sleds.
The boys were after him because he was a Jew.

At last his father and mother slept. He got up and dressed.
In the hall he took his sled and went out on tiptoe.
No one was in the street. The slide was worn smooth and
    slippery—just right.

He laid himself on the sled and shot away. He went down only
    twice.
He stood knee-deep in snow:
no one was in the street, the windows were darkened;
those near the street-lamps were ashine, but the rooms inside
    were dark;
on the street were long shadows of clods of snow.
He took his sled and went back into the house.


21

Grandfather was growing blind. He sat in his chair beside the
    window.
He went out of the house only on holy days—to synagogue.
Rosh Ha-Shonoh the boy led him to Brownsville, both afraid.
Nothing happened. But on the way back a boy, driving a
    grocer's wagon, drove near them
and leaning out, cracked his whip above their heads.

Yom Kippur Uncle went with Grandfather.
It was night and they had not come. They should have been
    home by twilight to break their fast.
The boy went down to the stoop to wait.
Grandfather was coming alone.
"Where's Uncle?" Grandfather did not answer. In his hurry
    upstairs he stumbled.
He went to his chair beside the window and sat looking into
    the night.
Tears rolled out of his blind eyes and fell upon his hands.
Uncle came, bare-headed, blood oozing out of his hair.


22

His sickness over, he was still abed.
He saw through the window when it was unfrosted,
clouds and a tree's branch.
Birds crossed the sky,
or a sparrow hopped from twig to twig.
He watched, becoming quiet as the branch;
it seemed to him that his blood was cool as sap.
When he moved hands or body, he moved slowly,
the branch's way at twilight.
His parents thought merely that he was still weak.

March he was well. Often when he came into his room,
he went to the window for a few minutes and stood watching
     the tree.
So he watched it bud and the little leaves and the leaves grown
     large and the leaves color and fall.

His parents had lost their money. They sold the house and
     were to move away.
He went up to his room for the last time.
The trunk of the tree, branches and twigs were still.
He thought, The tree is symmetrical . . . and whatever grows
     . . . in shape . . . and in change during the years. So is
     my life . . . and all lives.
He went down the stairs singing happily.
His father said, "There's so much trouble—and he sings."

## 23

At six o'clock it was pitch-dark. It might have been after
     midnight in the city and no lamps lit along the streets.
He would have liked to hide in the city from that sky of stars.
Beside bushes and thin, leafless trees he walked upon the
     frozen clods and ruts.
There was no wind across that blackness of fields and lakes;
only the sound of his own feet knocking on the road.
There the stars were poured, and there scattered. He thought,
The symmetry in growth and life on earth, our sense of order,
     is not controlling in the universe.

## 24

Their boarder had come to America before his wife and
     children.
He sat at the table working at a beginner's book in English.
In a moment of pity she began to teach him.
Once, when her mother was out marketing, he took hold of
     her hand and fondled it.
She snatched it away. She tried to go on with the lesson as if
     nothing had happened,
but for some time she could feel her heart pounding.
She decided to tell her mother nothing because it might worry her.
Maybe it was just a way to show his thanks. Besides, she was
     ashamed.

47

The next night he sat down to his lesson as if nothing had
    happened;
the lessons went on smoothly even with her mother away.

One evening she almost danced about the kitchen at her work:
    they had taken their last examination that morning,
school would soon close, and the summer vacation begin.
In the afternoon she had gone to Central Park. The girls raced
    over the meadow, noisy as birds at dawn.
After supper she and the boarder sat down to their lesson.
The color in her face and eyes had deepened. She smiled and
    held her face close to his in her eagerness to teach.
Her mother was going out to get a mouthful of fresh air after
    her day in the shop.
"It's so nice in the street, why don't you come?" "I'll be soon
    through, Mamma."
His hand was resting on the back of her chair. He pressed her
    to him. She tried to free herself
and drew her head back. He kept kissing her throat, his hands
    trying to pin down her arms.
Suddenly she was limp. He let go. She was looking at him,
    her mouth open, gasping.
She had pushed back her chair and was running out of the
    door.
She wondered that she was not falling she went down the
    stairs so fast.

25

The trees at the end of the lawn were still as cliffs.
He could see a bit of the moon, a white pebble embedded in
    the blue sky.

On the hour the bell in Switzler Hall tolled.
The strokes sank into the stillness of the afternoon.

For a while in the sunny paths that led to the colleges,
too far away to have their speech or steps on the gravel heard,
girls and men were walking.
Lying on the warm grass he rhymed:

*Love, let us lie down here*
*on the warm grass,*

*glad that we are so near.*

*Watch on the shores of sleep*
*the still waves pass,*
*feel that sea's languid air*
*move in our hair,*

*and turn at times to trace*
*in quiet wise,*
*each other's smiling face*
*and sleepy eyes.*

## 26

He woke in the dawn and saw in front of the house the
    treetops and pale sky beyond,
the darkness between the trees fading, and then the trees clear
    in the fresh blue day.

The dew lay in large drops over the grass beside the walk.
Birds were hopping about, robins large among the sparrows,
and from the bay gulls swung silently overhead.

The smell of coffee filled the screened porch. Her glance bid
    him welcome.
The sunlight edged its way along, and when she walked
    through it,
her yellow hair and the white flesh of her hands shone.

## 27

On the counter were red slabs and rolls of beef. Bolognas hung
    along the walls and from the ceiling.
He carried his sliced bologna and two cents worth of bread to
    a table.
She came in and flung her muff upon the table, almost upon
    his bread.
Waiting to be served, she stood in front of the mirror,
smoothing her dress over her hips, curving her arms to her
    hair, stretching herself.
She sat down facing him, smiled, and soon they were
    talking.
When she had gobbled her food, he gave her some of his.

He was through and still he sat there, warming himself at her
   quick beauty.
He had but to ask and he knew that she would come along.
He arose and went out. He walked down the street slowly,
   asking himself if he wasn't a fool.


28


His mother stepped about her kitchen, complaining in a low
   voice;
all day his father sat stooped at a sewing machine.
When he went to high school Webber was in his class.
Webber lived in a neighborhood where the houses are set in
   lawns with trees beside the gutters.
The boys who live there, after school, take their skates and
   hockey sticks and play in the streets until nightfall.
At twelve o'clock the boys ran out of school to a lunchroom
   around the corner.
First come, first served, and they ran as fast as they could.
Webber would run up beside him and knock him against the
   wall.
He tried not to mind and thought Webber would tire of it.
One day he hit Webber's side; his fist fell off Webber's over-
   coat. Webber turned with a glad shout and punched him
   as he cowered.
His home was in a neighborhood of workingmen where there
   were few Jews.
When he came from school he walked as quickly as he could,
his head bowed and cap pulled low over his face.
Once, a few blocks from home, a tall lad stopped him.
"Are you a Jew? I knock the block off every Jew I meet."
   "No," he answered.
"I think you're a Jew. What's your name?" He told him,
glad that his name was not markedly Jewish and yet foreign
   enough to answer for his looks.
"Where do you live?" He told him and added, "Come around
   any old time and ask about me." So he got away.
When he was through high school he worked in the civil
   service as a typist, taken on until a rush of business was
   over.
He took the test for a steady job, but his standing on the list
   was low,
unlikely to be reached for a long time, if ever before the new list.

Looking for work, he always came upon a group waiting for
    the job.
He was short and weak-looking, and looked peevish. He could
    not get work for months.
At last an old German storekeeper wanted to hire him and
    asked at what he had been working. He told him.
"It doesn't pay me to break you in, if you are going to leave
    me. Have you taken another civil service test? Are you
    waiting for a new appointment?"
"No," he answered.
In a few months a letter came to his home from the civil
    service board, asking him to report for work as a typist, a
    permanent appointment.
There was no hurry, but his father did not know and so
    brought the letter to the store.

There had been a boy in his class at school whose name was
    Kore.
Kore was short, too, but he had the chest of an old sailor and
    thick, bandy legs. He shouted when he spoke and was
    always laughing.
Kore moved into the block. With Kore he was not afraid to
    stand on the stoop after work or go walking anywhere.
Once they went to Coney Island and Kore wanted to go
    bathing. It was late at night and no one else was in.
They went along the beach until they came to the iron pier the
    steamboats dock at.
Kore boasted that he would swim around the pier and slid
    away into the black water.
At last the people were gone. The booths were long darkened.
He waited for Kore at the other side of the pier, watching the
    empty waves come in.

## 29

## The Burden

The shop in which he worked was on the tenth floor. After six
    o'clock he heard the neighboring shops closing, the
    windows and iron shutters closed.
At last there was only a light here and there.
These, too, were gone. He was alone.
He went to the stairs.

Suppose he leaned over the railing.
What was to hold him back from plunging down the stairwell?
Upon the railway platform a low railing was fencing off a drop
    to the street—a man could step over.
When the train came to the bridge and the housetops sank and
    sank, his heart began to pound and he caught his breath:
he had but to throw himself through the open window or walk
    to the train platform, no one would suspect, and jerk
    back the little gate.
He would have to ride so to and from work. His home was on
    the third floor, the shop on the tenth. He would have to
    pass windows and the stairwell always.

## 30

In high school she liked Latin and the balances of algebra.
Her mother had died years before and her father married again.
The new wife was solicitous for her husband. "A workingman
    —has he the means for this education of a girl?"
They took her out of school and got her a job as a bookkeeper.

A student at one of the universities whom she had met in high
    school, began to call.
She herself had been reading, but evenings are too short;
    besides, her reading was haphazard.
They talked of books that he knew and what was good in his
    lectures. Her stepmother and father said, "It will be years
    before he'll finish his studies and make a living. When
    he'll be ready to marry, you'll be too old. He's wasting
    your time."
It was useless talking to her, but they spoke to him and he
    stopped calling.

A salesman, professionally good-humored, introduced him-
    self to her father. A good match, they all said. Besides,
    home was uncomfortable with a nagging stepmother.

## 31

### The Belly

When the boys next door practiced on the 'cello, he would
    draw up a chair and listen, pressing his palms against the
    wall as if to gather the sounds.

His mother would drive him away. "Do your lessons, you'll be
     left back again in school!"
But in the evening she would speak to her husband in Russian,
     so that the boy might not understand. "He is longing for
     it, let him take music lessons."
"Don't put such ideas into his head. Do I want my son to grow
     up a fiddler? Let him do his school work, why don't you
     see he's neglecting that?"

They thought that his father might make a man of him in
     business.
Gabriel liked to open and help lift the cases of cotton goods,
     to hammer nails into the cases they shipped and carry
     bundles to customers.
His father spoke kindly to him and told his mother, "He'll be
     all right after all."
He began to ask again for 'cello lessons. Spittle dripped from
     his father's lips. "What does he want of me?
If he wants to study, let him go to night school and take up
     bookkeeping, for instance.
I always wanted to study algebra, but what chance was there
     in Russia? Here the world is open for a young man.
But he has taken a notion to scratch on a fiddle into his head
     and I can't hammer it out.
If he had a great talent—but where will he end up, a fiddler at
     weddings or in a theatre?"

A rich uncle came on a visit when Gabriel was twenty. They
     were out walking and Gabriel spoke to him.
His uncle answered kindly, "Do you know what I advise you:
     stay with your father and do your best in the business;
     your father wants to do the best for you.
If he sees you're willing and capable, he'll take you into the
     firm. Then, when you're established and make a com-
     fortable living, take up whatever side-line you want to,
     music or anything else;
as long as you're dependent on your father, you must obey."
     "At that time, Uncle, I'll be too old to begin my music."
     "One is never too old to learn."

He saved some money from his allowance and left home. He
     priced 'cellos.
He did not want to work for any of the cotton merchants and
     meet his father.

He had found no job and all his money was spent.

He had not eaten that day and could not sleep at night.

When day came he fell asleep and woke at noon.

Holding on to the banisters, he walked down the stairs of the
lodging house. He began to walk along the street, his head
light as if it were a balloon.

Each step was a distance. He sat on stoops to rest. If no stoop
was near, he sat down on the curb-stone.

When he reached home, he tried to walk upstairs, but afraid
of fainting, he went up on hands and knees.

## 32

He was afraid to go through their grocery store, where his
father was still talking to customers. He went through the
tenement hallway into the room where they ate and slept,
in back of the store.

His little brothers and sisters were asleep along the big bed. He
took the book which he had bought at a pushcart, to read
just a page or two more by the dimmed gaslight.

His father stood over him and punched his head twice,
whispering in Yiddish, "Where have you been lost all day, you
louse that feeds on me? I needed you to deliver orders."

In the dawn he carried milk and rolls to the doors of customers.
At seven he was in his chum's room. "I'll stay here with
you till I get a job."

He worked for a printer. When he was twenty-one he set up a
press in a basement. It was harder to pay off than he had
thought.

He fell behind in his installments. If they took the press away,
he would have to work for someone else all over again.

Rosh Ha-Shonoh he went to his father's house. They had been
speaking to each other again for years.

Once a friend had turned a poem of his into Hebrew. It was
printed in a Hebrew magazine. He showed it to his father,
and his father showed it around to the neighbors.

After dinner his father said, "Business has been good, thank
God. I have saved over a thousand dollars this year. How
have you been doing?"

"Well." "But I hear that you need money, that you're trying to
borrow some?" "Yes." His father paused.

"I hope you get it."

54

## 33

Passing the shop after school, he would look up at the sign
and go on, glad that his own life had to do with books.
Now at night when he saw the grey in his parents' hair and
heard their talk of that day's worries and the next:
lack of orders, if orders, lack of workers, if workers, lack of
goods, if there were workers and goods, lack of orders
again,
for the tenth time he said, "I'm going in with you: there's more
money in business."
His father answered, "Since when do you care about money?
You don't know what kind of a life you're going into—
but you have always had your own way."

He went out selling: in the morning he read the *Arrival of
Buyers* in *The Times;* he packed half a dozen samples into
a box and went from office to office.
Others like himself, sometimes a crowd, were waiting to thrust
their cards through a partition opening.

When he ate, vexations were forgotten for a while. A quarter
past eleven was the time to go down the steps to Holz's
lunch counter.
He would mount one of the stools. The food, steaming
fragrance, just brought from the kitchen, would be
dumped into the trays of the steam-table.
Hamburger steak, mashed potatoes, onions and gravy, or a
knackwurst and sauerkraut; after that, a pudding with a
square of sugar and butter sliding from the top and red
fruit juice dripping over the saucer.
He was growing fat.

## 34

### Provided For

Her father and mother were anxious to see her married and
provided for as soon as possible.
Squat and ugly, her face pimpled, she was stupid and had just
managed to get through grammar-school, two years older
than her companions.
Her father wanted her to marry his clerk. He had a good-
looking, womanish face.

She used to say, "He's marrying me for money, he hates me!"

Her father bought him a store in the Italian quarter.
The man who sold the store had it for years and had made
    money.
Her husband despised Italians. When they would not buy, he
    lost his patience, glared or shouted.
He sniffed at the men when they came in after a day's ditching,
    cheated when he could and still could not make the store
    pay.

His father-in-law bought him a store in another neighborhood.
    He could not make a living and was always borrowing.
Once his father-in-law refused him more money.
He came home. The two elder children were in bed. His wife
    was suckling the baby. She stared out of the window,
    tears in her eyes.
He slapped her face. "Tell your father! And if he doesn't help
    me out—!"


35

### A Son with a Future

When he was four years old, he stood at the window during a
    thunderstorm. His father, a tailor, sat on the table sewing.
    He came up to his father and said, "I know what makes
    thunder: two clouds knock together."
When he was older, he recited well-known rants at parties.
    They all said that he would be a lawyer.
At law school he won a prize for an essay. Afterwards, he
    became the chum of an only son of rich people. They
    were said to think the world of the young lawyer.
The Appellate Division considered the matter of his disbarment.
    His relatives heard rumours of embezzlement.

When a boy, to keep himself at school, he had worked in a
    drug store.
Now he turned to this half-forgotten work, among perfumes
    and pungent drugs, quiet after the hubble-bubble of the
    courts and the search in law books.
He had just enough money to buy a drug store in a side
    street.

Influenza broke out. The old tailor was still keeping his shop
and sitting cross-legged on the table sewing, but he was
half-blind.
He, too, was taken sick. As he lay in bed he thought, "What a
lot of money doctors and druggists must be making; now
is my son's chance."
They did not tell him that his son was dead of influenza.

## 36

In a month they would be married.
He sang a song to himself in which her name was the only
word.
His mother was waiting up for him. She said, "I was told today
that her mother died an epileptic,
and her brother is an idiot in a home somewhere. Why didn't
she tell you?"
He thought of hugging her narrow shoulders, comforting her;
of noting their children's quirks and screeches fearfully—
how the moonlight had been glittering in her eyes.

## 37

### A Deserter

Their new landlord was a handsome man. On his rounds to
collect rent she became friendly.
Finally, she asked him in to have a cup of tea. After that he
came often.

Once his mouth jerked, and turning, she saw her husband in
the doorway.
She thought, One of the neighbors must have told him.
She smiled and opened her mouth to speak, but could say
nothing.
Her husband stood looking at the floor. He turned and went
away.

She lay awake all night waiting for him.
In the morning she went to his store. It was closed.
She sent for his brothers and told them he had not been home.
They went to the police. Hospitals and morgues were
searched. For weeks they were called to identify drowned
men.

His business had been prosperous; bank account and all were
   untouched. She and their baby girl were provided for.
In a few years they heard of him. He was dead.
He had been making a poor living in a far off city. One day he
   stepped in front of a street-car and was killed.

She married again. Her daughter married and had children.
   She named none after her father.

38

At night, after the day's work, he wrote. Year after year he
   had written, but the right words were still not all there,
   the right rhythms not always used. He corrected the old
   and added new.
While away on a business trip he died. His children playing
   about the house, left home by the widow out at work,
   found the manuscript so carefully written and rewritten.
The paper was good to scribble on. Then they tore it into bits.
   At night the mother came home and swept it out.

39

When at forty he went to America, the family was glad to be
   rid of him, envious and quarrelsome. All but him had
   married and were well-to-do.
The smallpox when a child had left him ugly. Because it had
   also left him sickly, he had been humored in not going to
   school, and so could not read or cypher.
To strengthen him he had been apprenticed to a blacksmith.
When he walked he kept hitching up his shoulders and
   throwing out his hands.
He spoke indistinctly and so foolishly that when understood,
   his hearers could not help smiling. Sure that they did not
   understand, he would repeat what he had said until tears
   were in his eyes.

In New York he stayed with a pushcart pedlar. The pedlar had
   a daughter who had worked her way through high school
   and was in college.
The blacksmith's arm became infected and he could not work.
He stayed at home waiting for his arm to heal, silently
   watching as she moved about the house or did her lessons.
   She tried not to mind his eyes always on her.

At last she insisted that he move away. So he had to take
    lodgings elsewhere.

After supper he would stand in front of the house in which she
    lived, hoping that she would come out on an errand.
The boys playing in the street, discovered him, and searched
    the gutters for peach pits and apple cores
to throw over their shoulders at him as they passed, intent
    upon the sky.
He would chase them in his jerky way.

## 40

As he read, his mother sat down beside him. "Read me a little."
"You wouldn't understand, Ma." "What do you care? Read me
    a little.
When I was a girl I wanted to study so much, but who could?
My father used to cry when I talked to him about it,
but he cried because he couldn't afford to educate the boys—
    even."
As he read, she listened gravely; then went back to her
    ironing.
The gaslight shone on her round, ruddy face and the white
    cotton sheets that she spread and ironed;
from the shelf the alarm-clock ticked and ticked rapidly.

## 41

He had a rich uncle who sent him to a university and would
    have taken him into the firm; but he went off and married
    a girl, the men of whose family were truckmen.
His uncle would have nothing to do with him, and he became
    a cigar pedlar; but his wife was beautiful.
Even after she had borne children and had had to drudge and
    scrimp all her married life, whenever she came to his
    lodge ball, men and women turned to look at her.

His uncle died and left him a little money. And just in time,
    because he was growing too old to walk around at his
    business the way he had to.
He bought a formula for making an oil, rented a loft in which
    to manufacture, hired a salesman.

Perhaps the formula was a swindle, perhaps it was lack of
  experience in the business, but in a year or two he lost his
  money.
He went back to cigar peddling. His wife's hair had become
  white, but it gave her new beauty.

## 42

His father carved umbrella handles, but when umbrella
  handles were made by machinery, there was only one
  man for whom his father could work.
The pay was small, though it had once been a good trade.
They lived in the poorest part of the ghetto, near the lots
  where people dump ashes.
His father was anxious that his son should stay at school and
  get out of the mess he himself was in. "Learning is the
  best merchandise," he would say.
His father died; there was his mother to be taken care of. He
  taught in a school in the ghetto.
Some pupils came at nine and stayed until three; others came
  after public school and stayed until evening; most of the
  pupils came in the evening.
The courses were crammed, lasting a few months, pupils and
  teachers anxious to be rid of the matter as soon as
  possible.
So he worked day and night, week-days and Sunday.

His mother was dead. It was cold in the street and windy. A
  dry snow had fallen and the feet of the walkers were
  turning it into brown sand.
He was forty.
Now he was free. To do what? He knew no one whom he
  cared to marry. And who would go into his poverty?
If he were to give up this work he knew so well, to what else
  could he turn?
He would just keep on. He had lost this world and knew there
  was no other.

## 43

### The Lawyer

A man made cloaks of material furnished. The man for whom
  the cloaks were made refused them: defects in the

material. But the material was yours. But the defects were
   shown by white strings in the selvage; your cutter should
   have avoided them.
A woman fell downstairs; no light in the hallway. There was!
   but boys stole the electric bulbs. The janitor was told; he
   should have lit the gas.
Water from the chop-suey joint upstairs came through the
   ceiling upon our silk. The water fell on a table where it
   damaged nothing; they took their silk, gone out of style,
   and dabbled it in the water. The silks were on the table to
   be cut.
Our union takes steam-shovel engineers only, but their union
   takes all kinds; they want to put us out of business. One
   of our men was on a job; they call out the locomotive
   engineers and make the boss—
Why was he spending his life in such squabbles?

## 44

Both daughters had married well; their husbands earned
   enough, and more each year.
Her husband's business was good and they had as much as two
   elderly people wanted.

Her younger daughter died in childbed.

Her husband had gone to his store long before.
She wrapped her head and shoulders in her shawl, knitting her
   thoughts.
She got up at last and poured herself some brandy.
When she went out she took a brandy flask in her bag to nip
   in lavatories.

Her other daughter died in childbed.
Her son-in-law married again. The new wife took the elder
   children from school and sent them to work.
They became coarse; their house was full of quarreling.

Their grandmother was now in an asylum.
Her husband came to see her. Once he saw the lunatic children
   playing in the yard.
"Why do you cry?" she asked. "You cry for them, but not
   for me . . .

I am sharpening a knife to kill my grandchildren, but not you:
    you must pay for my board here."

## 45

He had a house of his own and a store. His wife took care of
    the store, and he at home studied Torah and Talmud.
His store was burned down. In those days they were not
    insured, but still he had the house.
He rented all of it but a room where he stayed and studied.
Once, when he was saying the morning prayer, Mendel, one
    of his tenants, came to him and said, "My son, the
    lawyer, has been arrested; won't you sign his bond here?"
It was not a bail bond but a deed; and in a few months
    Mendel made him move out of the house.
He went to a lawyer. The lawyer told him, "We can get the
    house back easily."
"What will they do to Mendel?" "Send him to Siberia."
    "Would it be right for me to put a Jew into the hands of
    *goyim*?"
He had to give children lessons in Hebrew. His son became a
    glazier. While working in another town his son died.
His daughter-in-law baked *begel* and his grandchildren sold
    them in the streets.

One day Mendel came to ask forgiveness.
He, too, had lost his money, and his son, too, the lawyer, had
    died.
He turned his face from Mendel; and so they stood, two old
    men.

## 46

When the club met in her home, embarrassed, she asked them
    not to begin: her father wanted to speak to them.
The members whispered to each other, "Who is her father?"
"I thank you, young men and women," he said, "for the
    honor of your visit. I suppose you would like to hear
    some of my poems." And he began to chant.

47

## The Doctor's Wife

The neighbors called her *die Schiesterka*—the shoemaker's wife.
She was squat, her speech coarse as their own.
People are always moving in and out of tenements;
the newcomers learnt the name and passed it on to others
who moved in afterwards, and all liked to use it.

She and the children were going to the country.
She had on a new waist, starched white and stiff,
and kept rubbing her red, sweating face with a handkerchief.
The doctor waved his hand from the stoop, and turned back
    to the office, now still and empty.

The conductor raised a hullabaloo about Minnie,
and she and Minnie raised such a hullabaloo back
that when full fare for Minnie was paid,
the conductor was too tired to argue about the others.
The ride became tiresome, babies cried, the windows had to be
    closed to keep out the cinders—
and opened because it became hot.
They reached their station at last. The boarding-house keeper
    had a buggy waiting.
"Drink the fresh air, children," she shouted,
"drink, drink, *ach gut!* If only Papa was here!"

48

The shoemaker sat in the cellar's dusk beside his bench and
    sewing-machine, his large, blackened hands, finger tips
    flattened and broad, busy.
Through the grating in the sidewalk over his window, paper
    and dust were falling year by year.

At evening Passover would begin. The sunny street was
    crowded. The shoemaker could see the feet of those who
    walked over the grating.
He had one pair of shoes to finish and he would be through.
His friend came in, a man with a long, black beard, in shabby,
    dirty clothes, but with shoes newly cobbled and blacked.
"Beautiful outside, really the world is beautiful."

A pot of fish was boiling on the stove. Sometimes the water
bubbled over and hissed. The smell of the fish filled the
cellar.

"It must be beautiful in the park now. After our fish we'll take
a walk in the park." The shoemaker nodded.

The shoemaker hurried his work on the last shoe. The pot on
the stove bubbled and hissed. His friend walked up and
down the cellar in shoes newly cobbled and blacked.

# V
# Five Groups of Verse
# 1927

*Five Groups of Verse* was published by the author in 1927 from 5 West Fourth Street, New York, and dedicated "to Albert Lewin in token of his help." The colophon reads:

> I set the type by hand and did the press work.
> 375 copies were printed and the type distributed;
> this is Number

C. R.

In addition to the revised versions of the poems from the four earlier books of verse (Reznikoff had also by now published three volumes of plays), the collection contained a fifth group of twenty numbered poems. These are printed here, with one revision made for the 1962 selection, *By the Waters of Manhattan* (see Appendix).

## 1

I charge you, lips and teeth,
keep watch upon my tongue:
silence is legal tender everywhere.

## 2

I have a quarrel with the clock.
*Quick, quick!*
These inconsiderable seconds fill
the basins of our lives to overflowing,
and we are emptied
into the sink and pipes of death.
How furiously it ticks this fine morning.
Sun, of all that lived God has only listened to Joshua,
how shall I hope that He will listen to me?

## 3

### Farquhar

#### I

*Margaret.* I have never regretted that my father gamed away
    his fortune
as much as I do, now that I have met George Farquhar.
I am convinced that were I wealthy he would marry me.
    *Her Friend.* How is he to know that you are not?
    *Margaret.* Not know the town's tattle?
    *Her Friend.* If there is tattle that you are penniless,
there may be tattle that you are rich
as a daughter of Hesperus—
    *Margaret.* What a subtle and ingenious mind you have,
    darling!—
    *Her Friend.* In whose estate
are quiet rooms where white Apollo smiles,
and penniless George Farquhar
may write comedies to outshine Congreve.
    *Margaret.* Excellent!
    *Her Friend.* You silly, should he bite and you two marry?
What are you to live by;
for Adam cannot delve nor this Eve spin?
    *Margaret.* Dearest, what *do* I live by?

The gratuities of friends.
If we marry, I am sure
of some happiness; for the rest,
I'll chance it—
I am my father's daughter.
Gossip until I have him caught
and my own, my very own.
     *Her Friend.* I'll talk your wealth, I'll make you rich—
in lies.
     *Margaret.* In love!

## II

*Margaret to Farquhar who has become consumptive.*
     O my dear, my dear, you were so dear to me
that  I threw my arms about your neck
and pulled you down.
Darling, it is I who have done this to you:
my kisses have sucked away your breath.
What friends we had among the rich and great!
But when we married and had most need of friends,
they left us to befriend each other . . .
I am unlucky;
my father was unlucky, too.
I know there is no meeting of the dead:
that we should be together once again—
oh, that would be too lucky for the like of me!

## 4

## Established

## I

*The music within the house is loud, the dancing swift. Outside*
     *A Woman.* This one still peddling, this one's son—a thief!
This one dead and that one dead,
but she's done well.
     *Another Woman.* She worked hard.
     *A Third Woman.* What's going on?
     *The First Woman.* She's marrying off her younger daughter.
Now both children are married—
married well.
The elder daughter has two children and soon—a third.
The grandchildren will not have to start where she did.

*The Second Woman.* She worked hard; now she eats the
   fruit of it.

## II

*A Woman.* Who's dead?
*Another.* I don't know.
*The First Woman.* Do you live on this block? Who's dead?
*A Third Woman.* A woman died in childbed.
*The First Woman.* What a heavy tread on the stairs! . . .
They are bringing down the coffin.

## III

*A Woman.* He is marrying again.
*Another.* So soon?
*The First Woman.* Why not?
Her children—
these need a mother.
*The Second Woman.* But their grandmother?
*The First Woman.* If in a drawer
she finds a trinket that her daughter used to wear,
or in a grandchild's face
sees her dead daughter and begins to cry—
the children have had enough of sorrow.

## IV

*A Woman.* Who's dead?
*Another.* I don't know.
*The First Woman.* Do you live on this block? Who's dead?
*Another.* A young woman. She died in childbed.

## V

*The Mother of the Dead Women.* I had this lump of lead
   before
when my father died,
but I was younger and my blood warm enough
to melt it away;
now it will weigh me down into the grave.
This lump of ice was here before,
but my blood when younger
could warm it into tears.

## VI

*A Woman to Another.* If their mother lived,

would they be sent to work?
What else can children become in shops and offices?
If at least home—
but their home!

5

## Autumn Night

The asphalt winds in and out
about the trees, the lawns, the lake;
a thousand lights shine among the trees,
and in the circles underneath
the grass is brightly green;
but all these lights do not warm the wind.

6

## Dawn

No one is on the lawn so early but the birds,
sparrows and robins pecking at the seeds
the wind has blown here; the wind itself is gone.

7

How miserly this bush is:
why do you crouch behind a fence,
holding on to your little copper leaves?
Have you no faith in spring?

8

From the fog a gull flies slowly
and is lost in fog. The buildings are only clouds.

9

## David

The shadow that does not leave my feet,
how shrunken now it lies;
with sunshine I am anointed king,

I leap before the ark, I sing;
I seem to walk but I dance about,
you think me silent but I shout.

10

## A Citizen

I know little about bushes and trees,
I have met them in backyards and streets;
I shall become disreputable if I hang about them.
Yet to see them comforts me,
when I think of my life as snarled.
Was not knowledge first on trees?

11

A star rides the twilight now,
all heaven to itself.

12

## A Sunny Day

The curved leaves of the little tree are shining;
the bushes across the street are purple with flowers.
A man with a red beard talks to a woman with yellow hair;
she laughs like the clash of brass cymbals.

Two Negresses are coming down the street;
they munch lettuce
and pull the leaves slowly out of a bag.

The pigeons wheel in the bright air,
now white, now the grey backs showing.
They settle down upon a roof;
the children shout, the owner swings his bamboo.

## 13
### Building Boom

The avenue of willows leads nowhere:
it begins at the blank wall of a new apartment house
and ends in the middle of a lot for sale.
Papers and cans are thrown about the trees.
The disorder does not touch the flowing branches;
but the trees have become small among the new houses,
and will be cut down;
their beauty cannot save them.

## 14

How difficult for me is Hebrew:
even the Hebrew for *mother*, for *bread*, for *sun*
is foreign. How far have I been exiled, Zion.

## 15

I have learnt the Hebrew blessing before eating bread;
is there no blessing before reading Hebrew?

## 16

My thoughts have become like the ancient Hebrew
in two tenses only, past and future—
I was and I shall be with you.

## 17

God saw Adam in a town
without flowers and trees and fields to look upon,
and so gave him Eve
to be all these.
There is no furniture for a room
like a beautiful woman.

## 18

The sun shone into the bare, wet tree;
it became a pyramid of criss-cross lights,
and in each corner the light nested.

After I had worked all day at what I earn my living,
I was tired. Now my own work has lost another day,
I thought, but began slowly,
and slowly my strength came back to me.
Surely, the tide comes in twice a day.

## 20

## Samuel

All day I am before the altar
and at night sleep beside it;
I think in psalms, my mind a psalter.
I sit in the temple. From inside it
I see the smoke eddy in the wind;
now and then a leaf will ride it
upward and when the leaf has spinned
its moment, the winds hide it.
Against their hurly-burly
I shut the window of my mind,
and the world at the winds' will,
find myself calm and still.

The days in this room become precious to others also,
as the seed hidden in the earth becomes a tree,
as the secret joy of the bride and her husband becomes a man.

Whatever unfriendly stars and comets do,
whatever stormy heavens are unfurled,
my spirit be like fire in this, too,
that all the straws and rubbish of the world
only feed its flame.

The seasons change.
That is change enough.
Chance planted me beside a stream of water;
content, I serve the land,
whoever lives here and whoever passes.

# VI
## "Editing and Glosses"
### from
### By the Waters of Manhattan:
### An Annual
### 1929

In 1929 Reznikoff published what was intended to be the first of an annual series, though it had no successor. *By the Waters of Manhattan: An Annual* consisted of family memoirs in prose (later revised as part of *Family Chronicle* [1963]) and a section of verse workings of Old Testament sources, printed here from the first edition.

# ISRAEL

## I

Our eldest son is like Ishmael, Jacob is like you;
therefore, you like Esau better:
because he is a hunter, a man of the fields,
can bring you venison from distant cliffs,
is strong, and covered with hair like a ram;
but Jacob who is like you, a quiet man, dwelling in tents, is
    the better.
Esau is like a club, Jacob a knife,
Esau is stupid, Jacob shrewd,
Jacob is like my brother Laban.

My father, sit and eat of my venison.
How is it that you have found it so quickly?
God helped me.
Come near that I may feel you, my son,
whether you are my very son Esau or not;
the voice is Jacob's voice, but the hands are Esau's.
Are you my son Esau?
I am.
Come near now and kiss me, my son.

How dreadful are these cliffs!
I who have always lived in booths,
seldom far from the song of women at the doors,
or at the farthest, near the shepherd's flute—.
When Abraham's servant came to us,
he brought gifts of clothing, jewels of silver and gold;
you came with empty hands, it seemed;
but my cattle have been well cared for.
(Can Jacob match himself against Laban,
a young man who has nothing among strangers,
against a man grown grizzled among strong and crafty men?)

The seven years that I served for you, Rachel,
were but a few days.

Why have you cheated me?
In our place the younger is not given before the first-born.
Had Rachel been married first, the tears of Leah

would have made your marriage bitter.

When this beauty of which you keep telling me is gone,
as the petals are shaken from a tree—
surely, although they are so many, at last they have all
    fallen—
Leah now hires you of me with the mandrakes
her eldest finds in the field,
but who will find me anything in those days?

My companions so many nights,
physicians to whom I told my secrets,
I touch you:
you are wood;
so is the staff that helps us on our way,
the spoon that feeds us, and at last our coffin.
Does Laban among sons and brothers need you?
We need you,
a shepherd, women, children, and a flock of sheep,
among the mountains in the wilderness. (*She steals the idols.*)

Why have you stolen away,
and carried away my daughters as if they were captives of the
    sword?
Why did you not tell me,
that I might have sent you away with mirth and songs,
with drum and harp?
Why did you not let me kiss my sons and daughters?
The daughters are my daughters, the children are my children,
    and the flocks my flocks,
all that you see is mine;
but what can I do to these, my daughters,
or to the children whom they have borne?

How unworthy I am of the kindness which you have shown
    me,
God of Abraham and Isaac,
for with my staff I crossed the Jordan,
and am now two companies.
Deliver me now from the hand of Esau!
And whose are the children?
My children.
And what meant the company I met?

To find favor in your sight.
I have enough. Let that which you have be yours.

Look, Joseph is coming, the master of dreams.
What do the camels carry?
Spicery and balm and myrrh to Egypt.
What profit shall we have in the death of our brother?
Lift him out of the pit and sell him to these for pieces of silver;
and dip his coat in a goat's blood,
and send it to our father,
and say, we have found this and do not know whether it is
        your son's coat or not;
and he will think a beast tore Joseph to pieces.

## II

Since Potiphar made you his overseer,
he has been blessed in house and field;
all that he has is in your hand,
and he knows of nothing but the bread that he eats.
And you in our house have become comely—
you were nothing but a bag of bones.
Come here!
Your cheeks were sunken so,
your eyes staring and your hair
dishevelled like this, like this.
Are not my hands soft?
You stepped as lightly as a deer,
as slim and graceful as a deer,
and held your head as proudly.
Sit here.
Kiss me.
Not so.
Oh, you don't know how to kiss.
Kiss me so.
Wet your lips and kiss me so.
Kiss my eyes, my throat,
now my mouth—
oh, you fool! You fool!

You are magicians and wise men at my feasts;
now, what is the meaning of my dreams?

"Have me in mind when it shall be well with you,
make mention of me to Pharaoh, and bring me out of this
      house;
for I was stolen from the land of the Hebrews;
and here also I have done nothing that they should put me into
      the dungeon."
Since then, two full years have passed, and until this day I
      have forgotten Joseph.

Therefore, let Pharaoh set a man, discreet and wise,
to appoint overseers, and these gather in the cities from the
      fields about them
grain in the good years against the years of famine.
Where can we find such a man?
I have no one discreet and wise as you.
You shall be over my house, and according to your word shall
      my people be ruled;
only I, on the throne, will be greater.
Clothe him in fine linen and put a gold chain about his neck,
he shall ride in the second chariot and all cry out before him,
      Bend the knee!

You are spies, you come to see the nakedness of the land.
No, my lord, we are not spies, we have come to buy food.
We are brothers, the sons of one man in Canaan.
And is your father yet alive?
He is.
Have you another brother?
We have.
We were twelve,
the youngest is with our father,
and one is no more.

My lord, we have brought you a present of the fruit of our land:
A little balm, a little honey, spicery and myrrh, pistachios and
      almonds.
Is your father well, the old man of whom you spoke? Is he yet
      alive?
Is this your youngest brother of whom you spoke?

Why have you rewarded evil for good? Where is the cup from
      which my lord drinks?
The man in whose hand the cup was found shall be my
      bondsman.

*80*

Now when I come to the servant your father and the lad is
    not with us—
his brother is dead, and he alone is left of his mother, and his
    father loves him—
let me remain instead of the lad, a bondsman to my lord.

Let every man go out but these.
I am Joseph.
Come nearer.
I am Joseph, your brother, whom you sold into Egypt.
And now be not grieved, nor angry with yourselves,
for I was sent before you to save us all alive;
you meant evil against me, but it was meant for good.
Go up to our father and say to him,
your son Joseph has become head of all Egypt;
without Joseph no man, except Pharaoh on the throne, lifts
    hand or foot throughout Egypt.
You have not thought to see his face and you shall see his sons
    also.
Come to him and you shall dwell in the land of Goshen—
and he shall be near me and his children and his children's
    children,
and bring all your flocks and herds and all that you have;
for there are yet five years of famine.
You shall tell my father of all my glory in Egypt;
you shall take wagons out of Egypt for your little ones and
    your wives, and bring our father and come;
and I will give you all the good of the land of Egypt.
I will establish my people like a pyramid,
no longer to be blown along like sand.

### III

Our lives are bitter with service in mortar and brick,
we whose fathers watched the flock of stars,
and had no Pharaoh but the sun. When he came,
they led their sheep to pasture at the pace of the lambs—
few and evil are the days of our lives.
We have built Pithom and Raamses. What are two
cities to Pharaoh?
We must build him many as the stars.

Why do you complain? The more you are afflicted,
the more you multiply, the more you spread abroad.

What have you become?
A shepherd in a wilderness.
Your hair is grey;
how much longer
before you attempt the dreams of your heart?
Deliver my people out of Egypt,
bring them out of that land to a good land,
a land of milk and honey, the land of your fathers.

What is this you have done? Who sent for you?
Before Pharaoh and his court come two shabby Hebrews and say,
Let our people go, we pray you, three days' journey into the
      wilderness,
to hold a feast to God.
Who asked you to speak for us?
No wonder Pharaoh's court burst into laughter;
we have heard how Pharaoh smiled, leaned forward and said,
Who is your God that I should listen to Him?
I know Him not.
Then you should have known enough to be silent,
but you must speak on;
until Pharaoh answered in anger,
Why do you loose the people from their work? Get to your
      burdens.
And he commanded his officer, Give the people no more straw
      to make brick,
let them gather straw for themselves;
and the number of bricks they did make, you shall lay upon them,
you shall not make it less,
for they are idle, therefore they cry, Let us go and sacrifice to
      our God.

We are scattered throughout Egypt to gather stubble for straw,
and the taskmasters are urgent,
fulfill your work, your daily tasks, as when there was straw.
We are beaten and the taskmasters demand of us,
Why have you not fulfilled your task both yesterday and
      today?
You are idle, you are idle, therefore you say, Let us go and
      sacrifice to our God.
Who asked you to speak for us? God judge you,
because you made us hateful in the eyes of Pharaoh and his
      servants,

and put a sword in their hand to kill us.

The God of the Hebrews sent us to say,
Let my people go to serve Me in the wilderness,
and Pharaoh did not listen.
In the morning, when Pharaoh came to his barge,
was not the river foul? Pharaoh turned and went into his
     house.
The fish in the river died, the Egyptians loathed to drink from
     the river,
the water was foul in vessels of wood and vessels of stone;
and they dug for water—they could not drink the water of the
     river.
Still Pharaoh would not let us go.
And the dust became lice throughout Egypt,
there were lice upon man and beast;
and the river swarmed with frogs.
The frogs came up into the houses and into the bedrooms and
     upon the beds,
and into the ovens and into the kneading troughs.
Still Pharaoh would not let us go.
The frogs gathered themselves into heaps and the land stank;
and swarms of flies came into the houses
upon Pharaoh and his servants and his people—
the air was black with flies.
Still Pharaoh would not let us go.
Then a murrain was upon the cattle in the field,
upon the horses, upon the asses, upon the camels, upon the
     herds, and upon the flocks,
and the cattle died; boils broke out upon men;
it thundered and rained hail and fire ran down into the earth,
and the hail struck every man and beast in the field,
every herb of the field, and broke every tree;
the flax and barley were struck down,
for the barley was in the ear and the flax was in bloom.
And still Pharaoh would not let us go.
And an east wind blew all day and all night,
and in the morning brought the locusts;
they covered the earth so that the land was darkened
and ate what had escaped the hail,
every herb of the land and all the fruit of the trees—
not a blade or a leaf or anything green was left.
Still Pharaoh would not let us go.

Now there has been darkness throughout Egypt for three days
so that men grope in the darkness.
Let us go,
with our young and old, with our sons and daughters,
with our flocks and herds to hold a feast to our God, as He
    commanded us.

The water of the river has been foul before.
Then there were lice and frogs, flies, and a murrain upon the cattle,
and boils upon men. What have these to do with it—or their God?
It has hailed in Egypt before the Hebrews were here;
we have known locusts often enough and darkness.
Why do you come before me as magicians and charmers?
Are we Hebrews to believe this?
See my face no more. The day you see my face again,
you die. Drive them from me.

The first-born of the Egyptians die,
from the son of the Pharaoh upon the throne
to the son of the servant behind the mill,
to the son of the prisoner in the dungeon;
not a house among them is now without its dead!
You hear the cry throughout Egypt;
now take your flocks and herds, the jewels of silver and the
    jewels of gold,
the fine clothing you have borrowed from the Egyptians,
your young and old, your sons and daughters,
take the dough before it is leavened,
the kneading-troughs upon your shoulders,
and hurry out of this land!

Why did you take us away to die in the wilderness;
were there no graves in Egypt?
Did we not say to you, Let us alone;
was it not better for us to serve in Egypt than to die in the
    wilderness?

The Egyptians turn, they turn, they cannot drive!
Their chariot wheels are bound with sand!
The waters return, return upon the Egyptians,
upon the horses and the chariots;
Pharaoh's host and his captains are sunk in the sea!

The water is bitter, we cannot drink it. The water is bitter.
Is there only the bitter for us from which to choose?
The water is bitter, we cannot drink it.
The water is bitter. The water is bitter, we cannot drink it.

That we had died in Egypt,
when we sat by the fleshpots, when we ate bread to the full.
I remember the fish we did eat for nothing in Egypt.
The cucumbers and the melons, the onions, the leeks, and the
    garlic—
our soul is dried away;
there is nothing except this manna to look upon.

You are not to be like other nations;
you are to be a kingdom of priests, a holy nation.
You shall have no other gods besides Him;
you shall make no image,
or the likeness of anything in the heavens,
on the earth, or in the water,
to bow down to it and serve it.
By righteousness shall you serve God:
you shall not swear by his name falsely;
six days shall you do your work and on the seventh, rest,
in ploughing time and harvest you shall rest
that your ox and ass may rest and your servants;
honor your father and mother; you shall not kill;
you shall not whore; you shall not steal;
you shall not deal falsely with each other;
you shall not covet your neighbor's house,
your neighbor's wife, nor his manservant, his maidservant,
his ox, his ass, nor anything your neighbor's.
In righteousness shall you judge your neighbor:
you shall not respect the person of the poor nor honor the
    person of the mighty,
neither shall you favor a poor man in his cause.
If a witness has testified falsely,
as he thought to do to his brother, you shall do to him.
You shall put away evil from among you and your eyes shall
    not pity:
life for life, eye for eye, tooth for tooth, hand for hand, foot
    for foot,
burning for burning, wound for wound, stripe for stripe;
as a man does to his neighbor it shall be done to him.

You shall not follow a multitude to do evil,
you shall not go up and down, a talebearer,
you shall not hate your brother in your heart:
rebuke your neighbor,
but you shall not take vengeance, nor bear a grudge;
you shall love your neighbor as yourself.
If you meet your enemy's ox or his ass astray,
you shall surely bring it back;
if you see the ass of him who hates you lying under his burden,
you shall surely set it free.
You shall be holy men before God;
you shall make a distinction between the unclean and clean.
These you may eat: the ox, the sheep, the goat, the hart,
the gazelle, the roebuck, the wild goat, the antelope, and the
        chamois,
but not the camel, the coney, the hare, and the swine,
nor whatever beasts go upon paws,
nor whatever dies of itself,
nor of all that move in the waters,
whatever has not fins and scales;
and of those that fly, the flesh of these is an abomination:
the eagle, the vulture, the kite, the falcon, and every raven,
the ostrich, the sea-mew, the night hawk and the little hawk,
the cormorant, the great owl, the horned owl,
the pelican, the stork, the heron, the hoopoe and the bat;
and all creeping things,
whatever goes upon its belly or has many feet,
the weasel and the mouse, the great lizard, the gecko, the
        crocodile, the sand lizard and the chameleon.
When you come into the land that shall be yours,
and reap your harvest,
you shall not reap the corners of the field,
neither shall you gather the gleanings:
you shall not glean your vineyard,
neither shall you gather the fallen fruit;
you shall leave them for the poor and the wanderer.
The wages of a hired servant shall not remain with you all
        night until the morning;
you shall not muzzle the ox when he treads out the corn.
If a stranger comes among you, you shall not do him wrong;
the stranger shall be as the home-born among you,
you shall love him as yourself;

for you know the heart of a stranger, you were strangers in
    Egypt.
You shall do no unrighteousness in measures of length, of
    weight, or of quantity:
you shall have just balances, just weights, a just ephah, and a
    just hin.
When you go out to battle and see horses and chariots and a
    people more than you,
the officers shall say,
What man has built a house and has not dedicated it?
Let him return lest he die in the battle and another dedicate it.
What man has planted a vineyard and has not used the fruit?
Let him return lest he die in the battle and another use the
    fruit.
And what man has betrothed a wife and has not taken her?
Let him return lest he die in the battle and another take her.
What man is faint-hearted?
Let him return lest his brother's heart melt as his.
Six years you shall sow and reap;
the seventh year you shall let the land lie fallow
that the poor may eat and what they leave the beast of the
    field shall eat.
The poor will never cease:
therefore, I command you,
you shall open your hand to your brother—enough for his
    need.
If your brother be sold to you and serve you seven years,
at the end of the seventh year you shall set him free,
and you shall not let him go empty-handed:
you shall furnish him out of your flock and out of your
    threshing-floor and your wine-press,
as you have been blessed you shall give,
you shall remember that you were a bondsman in Egypt.
At the end of every seven years,
the creditor shall release that which he has lent:
he shall not exact it of his neighbor.
And you shall number seven sabbaths of years, seven times
    seven years,
then you shall sound the trumpet throughout the land
and shall hallow the fiftieth year and proclaim liberty to all
    the inhabitants:
it shall be a year of jubilee.
The land shall not be sold forever: the land is God's,

you are strangers and sojourners before Him;
you shall grant a redemption for the land;
but if the land is not redeemed,
it shall stay with him who bought it until the jubilee,
and in the jubilee he who sold it shall return to his possession.

You are not to do each what is right in his own eyes:
the words of this day shall be upon your heart,
teach them diligently to your children,
talk of them when you sit in your house,
along the way, when you lie down, and when you rise up,
bind them upon your hand,
they shall be frontlets between your eyes,
you shall write them upon the door-posts of your house and
    upon your gates.

# KING DAVID

"And David said to Solomon, 'My son, as for me, it was in my
mind to build an house unto the name of the Lord my God:
But the word of the Lord came to me, saying, Thou has shed
blood abundantly, and hast made great wars: thou shalt not build
an house unto my name, because thou hast shed much blood upon
the earth in my sight.' "

—I Chronicles XXII: 7, 8.

## I

His height was six cubits and a span;
his helmet brass,
the weight of his coat-of-mail is five thousand shekels of brass,
he had greaves of brass upon his legs,
and a target of brass upon his shoulders;
the staff of his spear is like a weaver's beam,
the weight of his spearhead is five hundred shekels of iron.
He stood before our camp and shouted,
Am I not a Philistine and you servants of Saul?
Choose a man to fight with me;
if he is able to kill me, we are your servants,
if not, you are ours.
And we stood there, dismayed—
even Jonathan.
Now there had come to the camp a lad from Bethlehem,
whose three eldest brothers had followed Saul to battle:
the lad brought them parched corn, and loaves and cheese for
        their captain.
And he asked of the soldiers, Who is this Philistine that he
        should challenge the armies of the living God?
They told him how the king had said that he would enrich the
        man who killed the Philistine,
and give the man Michal—the king's daughter—for a wife;
and then the soldiers jeered at him and said, Do you think to
        kill him?
His eldest brother pushed through the soldiers and said,
What are you doing here?
With whom have you left our few sheep in the wilderness?
I know your naughtiness: you have come to see the battle.
The lad answered them all, I will go and fight with this
        Philistine,

and they reasoned with him: What are you thinking of?
You are only a lad
and he has been a man of war since his youth.
I will go with my staff and sling and the stones in my scrip.

Goliath called out, Am I a dog that you come against me with
    a stick?
Come on, and I will give your flesh to the birds of heaven and
    the beasts of the field,
but as he lifted his spear,
the lad took a stone and slung it, and it sank into Goliath's
    forehead.
At this we rushed upon the Philistines.
Jonathan
has given the lad his own robe, girdle, sword and bow;
now David shall stay among the men of war,
and be Michal's husband.

## II

### The Feast in Saul's House

  Tell us how Ehud stabbed the king of Moab,
or of Deborah,
of Gideon, Jephthah, or Samson.
Tell us of Jonathan!
Tell us again how the city of Dan was taken.

  The kings came and fought,
they took no spoil;
the river Kishon swept them away.
The stars fought from heaven,
from their courses they fought against Sisera.
Tell of it you that ride on white asses,
that sit on rich carpets,
or walk, far from the noise of archers, by the pools of water.
Sisera's mother is looking from her window.
She cries through the lattice,
Why is his chariot so long in coming?
Her women answer her,
yes, she answers herself,
Have they not found, are they not sharing the spoil?
A woman, two women to every man!

Micah said to his mother,
The silver taken from you, about which you did utter a curse—
I took it.
She said, Blessed be my son, and gave two hundred pieces of
    the silver
to the moulder to cast an image of God to stand in Micah's house.
Now there came to the hill country a young man,
a Levite looking for a place,
and Micah said to him, Stay with me, be my priest,
I will give you ten pieces of silver a year, a suit of clothes and
    your food;
the young man was content.
And Micah said, Now I know that God will be good to me,
for I have a Levite as my priest.
The Danites had sent five men to spy out the land and they
    lodged in Micah's house,
went on and came to a city, Laish,
and saw how the people lived there—quietly, far from other
    Sidonians.
And their spies told the Danites of Laish.
Six hundred of them set out with weapons of war and on the
    way passed Micah's house.
The five who had been there went in and took the image and
    said to its priest,
Be still!
But why not come with us and be our priest?
Is it better for you to be a priest in the house of one man or to
    a tribe of Israel?
And the Levite went along gladly.
Micah and his neighbors ran after them shouting,
and the Danites said, What is the matter with you?
He answered, You have taken away my God and my priest,
    and you ask me what is the matter?
A Danite answered him then, Let us hear no more from you;
    there are angry fellows among us,
and they may fall upon you and sweep you away and the lives
    of your household.
The Danites went on and came to Laish and killed all who
    lived there and set it on fire:
there was no one to save it, for it was far from Sidon,
and they had dealings with no one, but had lived—a quiet
    people—in their valley.
The Danites rebuilt the city and called it Dan.

Then Abner said, Tell us of Saul,
tell us how he went looking for his father's asses
and met Samuel and was anointed king;
how Saul saved the people of Jabesh-gilead from the
     Ammonites;
how he fought the Philistines,
not a sword or a spear in the hand of any of us—
did they leave us a smith in all Israel?—
our people had hidden themselves in caves and in thickets and
     in rocks and in pits,
the Philistines in three companies were pillaging the land,
and not a city was without its garrison of Philistines;
tell us about ourselves, for we are heroes too!

Now Jonathan, the son of Saul, said to the young man who
     carried his armour,
Come, let us go over to the Philistines' garrison.
The passes by which Jonathan went
were between crags on one side and crags on the other,
and the Philistines said, Look, the Hebrews are coming out of
     their holes.
And the men of the garrison called to Jonathan,
Come up to us and we will show you a thing or two;
he climbed up on his hands and feet—and they fell before him!
That first slaughter was of about twenty men
within as it were half a furrow's length in an acre of land;
there was a trembling in the camp, in the field, and among all
     the people,
the garrison and those going out to pillage trembled.
The watchmen of Saul looked and saw the multitude going
     this way and that,
and Saul said to his priest, Bring the ark of God;
but while Saul talked to the priest the tumult in the Philistines'
     camp went on and grew—
and we hurried to the battle!
The Hebrews who had come with the Philistines into their
     camp from the country about,
they, too, fought with Saul and Jonathan against the
     Philistines;
and those who had hidden themselves in the hills of Ephraim,
when they heard that the Philistines fled, followed them hard.

The evil spirit is in the king: he neither sees nor hears.

Let David play;
when David used to play,
the king would wipe his eyes upon his sleeves,
and be himself again.

When the women came out of the cities,
to meet us from the slaughter of the Philistines,
did you not hear them answer each other,
as they played upon the timbrels,
Saul has slain his thousands,
and David his ten thousands?
They said of David ten thousands
and of me only thousands;
can he have more except the kingdom?

What has he done? What is his wickedness?
He has done nothing that you should want his life!
    You lie, you rebel! you son of a rebellious woman!
Do I not know that you have chosen the son of Jesse to your
        own confusion
and to the confusion of your mother's nakedness?
As long as the son of Jesse lives upon the ground,
you will not be established nor your kingdom;
bring him to me at once for he shall die!
    Why should he die? What has he done?

## III

### Michal

The grave men who will write
the history of the kings of Israel and of the wars of God,
will not trouble to write of our happiness:
I had never hoped for a husband brave as Jonathan,
and handsomer than my father—
there is none like David among the young men.

What have I done that your father seeks my life?
God forbid! It is not so!
There is only a step between me and death:
as I sat before your father at meat—
in all that I have done have I not served him only?

Where is David?
He is sick.
Then we will bring him in his bed to the king. Let us in!
I cannot. He is sick.
Why have you fooled me and let my enemy escape?

## IV

His brothers and all his father's house have come to David,
and every one in distress and in debt,
every one discontented:
he is their captain;
and he and his band are now in the land of Judah—in the
    forest of Hareth.

If he is in the land at all,
I will search him out among all the thousands of Judah.

We heard that David is in the land of Ziph;
and that he was lurking in the wilderness of Maon,
and from there that he has slipped away to the strongholds of
    En-gedi—
on the rocks of the wild goats.

My lord, he and his band have escaped to the Philistines,
and found favor in the eyes of the king of Gath;
the king has given them a town in which to live.
They raid the Amalekites,
and leave not a man or woman alive to tell on them in Gath;
when the king asks, Where have you made a raid today?
David answers, In the south of Judah,
and so the king believes of him, He has made his people hate
    him.
    Hear, you Benjaminites,
will the son of Jesse give every one of you fields and vineyards,
and make you all captains of hundreds and of thousands,
that all of you have conspired against me,
and no one shows me that my son has made a league with the
    son of Jesse,
and none of you is sorry for me?

I saw the son of Jesse coming to Ahimelech the priest,
and Ahimelech inquired of the Lord for him

And we spent the night in talk upon your roof;
you showed me all the work before my hand;
though I hid among the wagons when the tribes were called
    together,
you searched me out and anointed me;
though I followed my oxen, ploughing my fields year after
    year,
the messengers of Jabesh-gilead came to me.
And all that I did since you know:
how I freed Jabesh-gilead from the Ammonites,
how I fought the Philistines and the Amalekites and ruled our
    people,
and had no rest, neither by day nor by night.
Now the Philistines come against Israel by hundreds and by
    thousands—
and Samuel answered, Why have you disquieted me and
    brought me up from the dead?
Why do you ask me, if God has gone from you and has
    become your foe?
He has torn the kingdom from your hand and given you to the
    Philistines;
tomorrow you and your sons shall be with me.

The seer was against him
and all the witches:
Saul and Jonathan are dead
on the field of battle,
on the field of defeat.
Accursed,
nevertheless
they went into battle,
Saul and Jonathan,
and died bravely.

The men ran and fell dead on Mount Gilboa,
and the Philistines followed hard upon Saul and his sons
and killed Jonathan.
The archers overtook Saul.
His head and armour are in the house of their idols,
his body is fastened to the wall of Beth-shan.
An Amalekite who was near the field of battle
to see what he could find
ran to tell David,

and brought him the crown that was on Saul's head,
and the bracelet that was on his arm.
David has taken the spoil that his band has gathered
and is sending it to the elders,
as presents to his friends in the cities,
that he and his may live again in Judah.

For he saved us from the Ammonites—
let us steal away Saul's body and the bodies of his sons
and bury them here in Jabesh-gilead.

## VI

### Ish-bosheth and Abner

Why have you taken my father's concubine?
Do you mean to be king in my stead?

Who made you king of Israel and Benjamin, if not I?
I am kind to your house not to give you up to the king of Judah.

Have I not heard how you sent a messenger to David
to make a league with him:
to bring him all Israel,
to say to the elders,
You have looked for David to be your king;
now do it,
for by him God will save Israel?
You have betrayed me, Abner!
But take care, you will meet a sudden death one of these days:
have you forgotten how you killed Joab's brother
when David's men and yours were playing by the pool of
    Gideon,
when they fought each other and caught each other by the
    head and sent their swords into each other's sides,
and you struck Joab's brother with the staff of your spear
so that the end of it came out behind his body and he fell
    down and died?
Do you think Joab has forgotten?
Do you think David's captain will let you become as great in
    David's court as here?

Joab knows that I called to the lad to turn away,

to catch one of the young men and take his armour;
that he would not, but turned neither to the right nor left but
    followed me—
but never fear for me, you unworthy son of Saul,
but for yourself,
that none of your captains
comes into your house as you lie upon your bed
and sticks his knife into the fat of your belly until the dirt
    comes out,
and cuts off your head to bring it as a gift to David.

Have you this in mind?

Not I.
I have no need to steal upon a man asleep or unawares.
But I have come not to quarrel, but with a piece of news:
David sends me word that I should bring him Michal, whom
    Saul gave him as his wife.
Now send for her that I may bring her to David;
we must humour the king of Judah—
and your father was unjust to take her away and give her to
    another.
Look at Paltiel,
whom Saul chose for a son-in-law;
look at the tears in his eyes.
What, are you afraid to draw your sword at the Lion of Judah?
Well, well,
we shall let you run beside Michal,
weeping all the way,
as we bring her to David.
But do not go a step beyond the border of Israel,
or David's sword may take a swift dislike to you
at the thought of the five sons she has borne you.

## VII

While I was away on this foray to bring spoil for my lord
    the king,
you feasted Abner and sent him away in peace!
And now I am told the king mourns for Abner!

And you sent messengers in my name after Abner;
and as he came back to Hebron, met him in the gate,

and took him aside as if to speak with him—and stabbed him!
The guilt fall upon you!
May your house never be without a leper or one that leans on
      a staff or one dead by the sword or one that lacks bread!
Put on sackcloth and mourn for Abner;
a prince and a great man has fallen today in Israel!


    You know Abner brought Michal to deceive you,
to find out all you do—.
    In the heat of the day we came to Ish-bosheth's house—
we were captains of his—
Ish-bosheth lay on his bed,
we came into the house as if to take wheat,
and cut off his head!
    Here is the head of Ish-bosheth, the son of your enemy, Saul;
God has avenged my lord the king today!
    When one told me among the Philistines, Saul is dead,
thinking to have brought me good news,
I killed him:
that was his reward for his news.
How much more should I do
to wicked men who have murdered a righteous man
in his own house and upon his bed?
Cut off their hands and feet,
and hang them up beside the pool in the garden;
bury Ish-bosheth's head in Abner's grave.


    Now, my lord, the elders of the tribes of Israel will come to
      you and say—
for they have neither captain left nor king—
they will say, We are your bone and flesh;
when Saul was king,
you led us out to battle and brought us back;
be our king.
See, my lord, God was with me when I struck Abner;
the enemies of my lord the king and all that rise against you
be as he is!


    And yet the Michal that I knew
with all the airs that suited Saul's daughter
and pleased me, newly from the sheepfold.
The sweat and fingerprints of another man upon her.

# VIII

I should like to see the mighty men David has:
I hear that they can use both the right hand and the left in
   slinging stones
and in shooting arrows from the bow;
that their faces are like the faces of lions,
and they are swift as the roes upon the mountains.

I should like to see Joab and Joab's brother, Abishai—
I have heard that when the Philistines were in Bethlehem,
David said, That I had a drink of the water of Bethlehem from
   the well by the gate;
and Abishai and two others broke through the Philistines'
   garrison,
and drew water out of the well and brought it to David;
but he would not drink of it and poured it out to the Lord,
for he said, Is not this the blood of those who risked their lives
   to bring it?

We have heard that Rizpah who was Saul's woman,
is under the tree on which the Gibeonites have hanged her
   sons and the five sons of Michal,
that she is there night and day
to drive away the birds of the air and the beasts of the field
that the birds do not rest on the dead by day nor the beasts
   tear them by night.
   Did not David himself say that the famine in the land was
      because of Saul and his bloody house,
because he massacred us, broke the covenant we have with
   Israel?
We want neither Saul's gold nor silver for atonement;
David himself gave us Saul's two sons by Rizpah and the five
   sons of Michal
to hang up to the Lord in Gibeah.

We are an embassy from the king of Hamath:
we have heard how you fought the Philistines
and have taken the bridle out of their hands;
how you have put garrisons in Syria and Moab and Edom and
   they have become your servants and brought you gifts;
and how you have fought the king of the Ammonites
and taken to Jerusalem their shields of gold;

my father, the king of Hamath, sends me to greet you and
    bless you,
and bring you vessels of gold, of silver, and of brass.

    The Lord took me from following the sheep
to be ruler of Israel,
and now He has given me rest from all my enemies.
Who am I, my God, and what is my house
that You have brought me so far?
I was surrounded
by the sorrows of death,
and the flood of ungodly men
frightened me;
I cried to my God!
He shot out His lightnings;
He took me
and drew me out of the deep waters.
By Him
I have run through a troop,
and jumped over a wall;
He teaches my hands war,
to bend the bow
He has given me my enemies:
I made them as dust before the wind;
I threw them away as dirt in the street.


IX

David and Michal

    God—
Who chose me rather than your father and all his house
to be king of Israel;
but you shall die childless.

    After you have hanged my sons,
from the eldest who was as tall as I
to the youngest who had not yet learned to walk:
this was my payment.
How much wiser was my father than his daughter or his son
    Jonathan!
    What did you want now with me,
an aging woman who has had five children?

Only the tarnished glory that still is Saul's,
that you should have Saul's daughter for a wife.
Did you expect the girlish body,
the young and cheerful face I had?—
I knew you would not care for me,
that I should never bear a child of yours,
that you had had a hundred women, a thousand women,
and had sent for me,
perhaps because the name of Saul was something still to you
        and your Jerusalem.
   Now I see when they say
you found Saul in a cave asleep and caught your servant's hand
that would have killed him—
it was no kindness—
you knew Saul's time would come;
if you had killed the Lord's Anointed,
there would have been war between you and Israel until your
        death.
And when you killed those who killed my brother Ish-bosheth,
you were the righteous man,
but you had all the profit of their wrong.
Joab you have not killed—who killed Abner—
Joab you need, you are afraid of Joab, he is your captain;
but Joab, too, will find you out some day, as I have found you
        out—
when his grey hairs go bloody to the grave.
   Your scribes will write you down a great king,
and of me—if they say anything at all—
but I belong to that doomed house of Saul
not even Jonathan could save.
I shall not weep before you again;
these tears are the last:
now I have wept them all away.
And I can speak of all my dead
without a tear.
Your scribes will write me down a cold, proud woman,
wandering about the garden of the king,
and you a glorious king, a glorious king.

# VII
# Jerusalem the Golden
# 1934

*Jerusalem the Golden* was published by the Objectivist Press from 10 West Thirty-sixth Street, New York, in 1934. The Press consisted of Reznikoff, George Oppen, and Louis Zukofsky. It was an outgrowth of Zukofsky's editorial work for the "Objectivist" number of *Poetry* (February 1931) and his *An "Objectivist" Anthology*, published in France in 1932 by George and Mary Oppen under the imprint "To Publishers." The editorial statement on the back of the dust wrapper was composed by Reznikoff; it reads:

> The Objectivist Press is an organization of writers who are publishing their own work and that of other writers whose work they think ought to be read.

The wrapper also listed an Advisory Board consisting of Ezra Pound and William Carlos Williams, with Zukofsky as "Sec'y." Already in 1934 the Press had published Williams' *Collected Poems*, with a preface by Wallace Stevens, and Reznikoff's prose work *Testimony*, with an introduction by Kenneth Burke.

*Jerusalem the Golden* bears the following epigraph and dedication:

TO MARIE
Sunt bona, sunt quaedam mediocra, sunt mala plura
Quae legis hic: aliter non fit, Avite, liber.
(Martial, Lib. I:XVI)

The acknowledgement thanks "the editors of *Contempo, Pagany, Poetry*, and *The Menorah Journal* for permission to reprint whatever they have used." The text that follows is that of the first edition, with a few revisions made for the 1962 selected poems, *By the Waters of Manhattan*. (For details see the Appendix.)

The Hebrew of your poets, Zion,
is like oil upon a burn,
cool as oil;
after work,
the smell in the street at night
of the hedge in flower.
Like Solomon,
I have married and married the speech of strangers;
none are like you, Shulamite.

2

## Hellenist

As I, barbarian, at last, although slowly, could read Greek,
at "blue-eyed Athena"
I greeted her picture that had long been on the wall:
the head slightly bent forward under the heavy helmet,
as if to listen; the beautiful lips slightly scornful.

3

The moon shines in the summer night;
now I begin to understand the Hebrews
who could forget the Lord, throw kisses at the moon,
until the archers came against Israel
and bronze chariots from the north
rolled into the cities of Judah and the streets of Jerusalem.
What then must happen, you Jeremiahs,
to me who look at moon and stars and trees?

4

Shameless moon, naked upon the cloudless sky,
showing your rosy and silver bosom
to all the city,

King Davids, we meditate business, and you
must now be bathing on a housetop in the pool of evening,
Bathsheba.

5

In a strange street, among strangers,
I looked about: above the houses
you were there, sole companion many a night—
the moon.

6

From my window I could not see the moon,
and yet it was shining:

the yard among the houses—
snow upon it,
an oblong in the darkness.

7

In the dark woods
the dark birds fly:
do you
with your single star, new moon,
come to light this darkness?

8

The wind blows the rain into our faces
as we go down the hillside
upon rusted cans and old newspapers,
past the tree on whose bare branches
the boys have hung iron hoops,
until we reach at last the crushed earthworms
stretched and stretching on the wet sidewalk.

9

On the hillside
facing the morning sun
how clear and straight each weed is.
On our way to the subway this morning
the wind blows handfuls of white petals upon us
from the blossoming tree on the hillside;
how like confetti—

but, of course,
this is the festival of spring.

## 10

These days the papers in the street
leap into the air or burst across the lawns—
not a scrap but has the breath of life:
these in a gust of wind
play about,
those for a moment lie still and sun themselves.

## 11

The river is like a lake this morning
for quiet—image of houses and green bank.

A barge is lying at a dock;
nothing moves but the crane
emptying the cargo.

The dark green hill,
the sunset, staining the river—
quiet as a lake;
the tree beside me
covered with white blossoms
that cover but cannot hide
the black gnarled branches.

## 12

At night walking along the streets, the darker because of trees,
we came to a tree, white with flowers,
and the pavement under the branches was white with flowers
    too.

## 13

On this beach the waves are never high:
broken on the sand bars, when they reach the shore—
a stranger might think the sea a bay
so gently do the waters splash and draw away.

The air is sweet, the hedge is in flower;
at such an hour, near such water, lawn, and wood,
the sage writing of our beginnings must have been:
lifting his eyes from the page he chanted,
"And God saw the earth and seas—that it was good."

14

This tree in the twilit street—
the pods hang from its bare symmetrical branches
motionless—
but if, like God, a century were to us
the twinkling of an eye,
we should see the frenzy of growth.

15

In the street I have just left
the small leaves of the trees along the gutter
were steadfast
in the blue heavens.
Now the subway
express
picks up speed
and a wind
blows through the car,
blows dust
on the passengers,
and along the floor
bits of paper—
wrappers of candy,
of gum, tinfoil,
pieces of newspaper . . . .

16

Going to work in the subway
this bright May morning
you have put on red slippers;
do they dance behind the counters
in the store, or about the machines
in the shop where you work?

## 17

Rails in the subway,
what did you know of happiness,
when you were ore in the earth;
now the electric lights shine upon you.

18

Walk about the subway station
in a grove of steel pillars;
how their knobs, the rivet-heads—
unlike those of oaks—
are regularly placed;
how barren the ground is
except here and there on the platform
a flat black fungus
that was chewing-gum.

19

**For an Inscription over the Entrance to a Subway Station**

This is the gift of Hephaestus, the artificer,
the god men say is lame.

20

In steel clouds
to the sound of thunder
like the ancient gods:
our sky, cement;
the earth, cement;
our trees, steel;
instead of sunshine,
a light that has no twilight,
neither morning nor evening,
only noon.

Coming up the subway stairs, I thought the moon
only another street-light—
a little crooked.

21

## Suburban River: Summer

In the clear morning
the gulls float
on the blue water,
white birds on the blue water,
on the rosy glitter of dawn.

The white gulls
hover
above the glistening river
where the sewers empty
their slow ripples.

22

The pigeon on the rocks has an anklet about each foot;
the feet slip a little on the granite.
The pigeon shrinks from the
spray
and peers into the
holes
between the rocks.

23

Upon a warm sunny afternoon in June,
where the water overflows the marble basins of the fountain,
the blue-black pigeons walk along the edges,
wading, and the spray ruffles their feathers.

24

## July

No one is in the street but a sparrow;
it hops on the glittering sidewalk,
and at last flies—into a dusty tree.

25

About an excavation
a flock of bright red lanterns
has settled.

26

The twigs of our neighbor's bush are so thin,
I can hardly see the black lines;
the green leaves seem to float in the air.

27

The bush with gaudy purple flowers is in the back yard—
seen only by its mistress, cats, and the white butterflies.

28

The cat in our neighbor's yard has convulsions:
from her mouth a green jet on the pavement—
she has added a leaf to their garden.

29

August

The trees have worn their leaves shabby.

30

Rhetoric

These streets, crowded an hour ago, are empty—
what crows that followed the armies of old
will be the scavengers?
The winds of night.

31

All day the street has been quiet.
Not a branch sways,
only the leaves of the corner tree twinkle.

32

The branches about the street-lamp
are so thick with leaves, it shines
only on a flag of pavement;
leaf behind leaf the night rings.

33

## September

The blue luminous sky furrowed into clouds; the clear air
crowded with rain—the dark harvest.

34

## After Rain

The motor-cars on the shining street move in semicircles of
    spray, semicircles of spray.

35

The morning light
is dim and blue—
the silent light
of woods;
but now begins
the slight yet multitudinous
noise of rain.

36

Along the flat roofs beneath our window
in the morning sunshine,
I read the signature of last night's rain.

37

See, your armor of scales, snake,
has not been good against this jagged rock,
and now you are coiled beside the walk,
pink flesh of your body showing,
and the sharp teeth of your open mouth.

## 38

Of our visitors—I do not know which I dislike most:
the silent beetles or these noisy flies.

39

What are you doing in our street among the automobiles,
horse?
How are your cousins, the centaur and the unicorn?

40

Rooted among roofs, their smoke among the clouds,
factory chimneys—our cedars of Lebanon.

41

## Suburb

If a naturalist came to this hillside,
he'd find many old newspapers among the weeds
to study.

42

Permit me to warn you
against this automobile rushing to embrace you
with outstretched fender.

43

From the middle of the pool
in the concrete pavement a fountain
in neat jets; the wind scatters it
upon the water. The untidy trees
drop their leaves upon the pavement.

44

## Lament of the Jewish Women for Tammuz
*Ezek. VIII:14*

Now the white roses, wilted and yellowing fast,
hang in the leaves and briers.

Now the maple trees squander their yellow leaves;
and the brown leaves of the oak have left Ur and become
    wanderers.

Now they are scattered over the pavements—
the delicate skeletons of the leaves.

45

Hunting Season

In the light of the street-lamp a dozen leaves
cling to the twigs of our tree for dear life;

an eager star is dogging the moon.

46

Feast, you who cross the bridge
this cold twilight
on these honeycombs of light, the buildings of Manhattan.

47

I thought for a moment, The bush in the backyard has
    blossomed:
it was only some of the old leaves covered with snow.

48

This smoky winter morning—
do not despise the green jewel shining among the twigs
because it is a traffic light.

49

A Garden

About the railway station as the taxicabs leave,
the smoke from their exhaust pipes is murky blue—
stinking flowers, budding, unfolding, over the ruts in the
    snow.

## 50

A black horse and a white horse, pulling a truck this winter
    day,
as the smoke of their nostrils reaches to the ground,
seem fabulous.

51

The dead tree at the corner
from the gray boughs of which the bark has fallen
in places and all the twigs—
be thankful, you other trees,
that, bare and brown, are only leafless
in a winter of your lives.

52

Now that black ground and bushes—
saplings, trees,
each twig and limb—are suddenly white with snow,
and earth becomes brighter than the sky,

that intricate shrub
of nerves, veins, arteries—
myself—uncurls
its knotted leaves
to the shining air.

Upon this wooded hillside,
pied with snow, I hear
only the melting snow
drop from the twigs.

53

Suburban River: Winter

The street lights
begin to shine
on the snow;
the river is
flowing

in cakes of ice;
from the luminous twilight
falls
a handful of snowflakes.

## 54

The days are long again, the skies are blue;
the hedges are green again, the trees are green;
only the twigs of the elms are dark.
At night the wind is cold again;
but by day the snow of your absence is melting:
soon May will be here and you the queen of the May.

## 55

You tell me that you write only a little now.
I wrote this a year or two ago
about a girl whose stories I had read and wished to meet:
*The traveller*
*whom a bird's notes surprise—*
*his eyes*
*search the trees.*
And when I met her she was plain enough.
So is the nightingale, they say—
and I am glad that you do not belong
to those whose beauty is all song.

## 56

Meeting often, we find we cannot meet enough,
and words are counterfeit, silence only golden,
and streets at night are beautiful.
I find the valentines are true, the hearts and arrows—
sighs and misty eyes; and the old poems—
I find them true.

## 57

It was in my heart to give her wine and dainties,
silken gowns, furs against the wind;
a woolen scarf,
coffee and bread was all that I could buy:

It is enough, she said.

It was in my heart to show her foreign lands,
at least the fields beyond the city:
I could not pay our way;
when she would see a row of street-lamps shining,
How beautiful, she would say.

58

You think yourself a woman,
because you have children and lovers;
but in a street
with only Orion and the Pleiades to see us,
you begin to sing, you begin to skip.

59

All day the pavement has been black
with rain, but in our warm brightly-lit
room, Praise God,
I kept saying to myself,
and saying not a word,
Amen, you answered.

60

Though our thoughts often, we ourselves
are seldom together.
We have told each other
all that has happened; it seems to me—
for want of a better word—that we are both unlucky.
Even our meetings have been so brief
we should call them partings, and of our words
I remember most "good-by".

61

Our nightingale, the clock,
our lark,
perched on the mantel,
sings so steadily:
O bird of prey!

*119*

The clock
on the bookcase ticks,
the watch on the table ticks—
these busy insects
are eating away my world.

My hair was caught in the wheels of a clock
and torn from my head: see, I am bald!

If you ask me about the plans that I made last night
of steel and granite—
I think the sun must have melted them,
or this gentle wind blown them away.

I once tore up a sapling to make myself a stick:
it clung to the earth, but I cut away its roots,
stripped off its twigs and bark;
a woman passing nodded her head as if to say, What a pity,
and I had no joy of the stick and threw it away.

If there is a scheme,
perhaps this too is in the scheme,
as when a subway car turns on a switch,
the wheels screeching against the rails,
and the lights go out—
but are on again in a moment.

The sun shining on the little waves of the bay, the little leaves
    of the hedge—
with these I school myself to be content.

### 68

The house is warm in winter, cool in summer;
but the cloth of the awning ripples and flutters,
the leaves of the shade tree are uneasy,
the twigs of the bushes keep nodding together.

### 69

Among the heaps of brick and plaster lies
a girder, still itself among the rubbish.

### 70

Out of the inexhaustible sea
the waves curve under the weight of their foam,
and the water rushes up to us;
the wind blowing out of the night,
out of the endless darkness,
blowing star after star upon the sky
out of the inexhaustible night;
wave after wave
rising out of the sea.

### 71

When the sky is blue, the water over the sandy bottom is
    green.
They have dropped newspapers on it, cans, a bedspring, sticks
    and stones;
but these the patient waters corrode, those a patient moss
    covers.

### 72

**The Evil Days**

The sun lights up
each mote upon the table,
but the old man
finds the page blurred
and lights the lamp.

## Asylum Product

Brown and black felt, unevenly stitched with purple thread;
what unhappiness is perpetuated in the brown and black of
    this pincushion,
lunatic?

## The English in Virginia, April 1607*

They landed and could
  see nothing but
  meadows and tall
  trees—
cypress, nearly three
  fathoms about at the
  roots,
rising straight for
  sixty or eighty feet
  without a branch.
In the woods were
  cedars, oaks, and
  walnut trees;
some beech, some elm,
  black walnut, ash,
  and sassafras; mul-
  berry trees in
  groves;
honey-suckle and
  other vines hanging
  in clusters on
  many trees.
They stepped on
  violets and other
  sweet flowers,
many kinds in many
  colors; straw-
  berries and rasp-

*Based upon the *Works of Captain John Smith*, edited by Edward Arber.

berries were on
  the ground.
Blackbirds with red
  shoulders were
  flying about
and many small birds,
  some red, some blue;
the woods were full of deer;
and running
  everywhere
  fresh water—
  brooks, rundles,
  springs and creeks.
In the twilight,
  through the thickets
  and tall grass,
creeping upon all
  fours—the
  savages, their
  bows in their
  mouths.

75

## Jeremiah in the Stocks
### An Arrangement of the Prophecies

Jeremiah, in the stocks in the gate of Benjamin, cried to the
princes of Judah, I have been born a man of quarrels—O
that I had a lodging-place in the wilderness that I might go
from my people! I sat alone because of the Lord; I found his
word and did eat it—it was to me joy and rejoicing. But I
was derided, all were sided against me, since I cried out—
cried violence and spoil! Then I said, I will not mention Him
any more, but bore His word like a fire shut up in my bones
—and could not keep still.

Then Pash-hur, the chief officer in the Lord's house, who had
placed Jeremiah in the stocks, faced the princes of Judah
sitting in the gate, and cried, This man should die because
he has lied and prophesied against this city, and has prophesied in the name of the Lord for the house of the Lord
the same end as Shiloh's! and, pushing aside those in the
muck about the stocks, struck Jeremiah.

And one of the princes said, Jeremiah, you Benjaminite, even your brothers, the priests in Anatoth, have said to you, Do not prophesy or you die by our hands; what then do you look for at the hands of others? If you have raced with the footmen and they outpaced you, how will you run beside horses? And if in the land of your dwelling in which you trusted—what will you do in the swelling of Jordan? And at this Pash-hur began to cry, This man should die! He must die!

One of the elders that stood beside the princes said, Micah prophesied in the days of King Hezekiah and spoke to all Judah, The pride of Zion shall be plowed like a field and proud Jerusalem become heaps. Did the king put him to death? King Hezekiah weeps, hears the Lord and fears the Lord and does justice before the Lord—until the Lord repented of what he was to do against Judah. Jeremiah shall not be given to the people to be put to death! And all the elders began to cry, He shall not die!

Pash-hur answered them, Uriah who prophesied against this city and against this land, according to all that Jeremiah had said, when he heard that the king was about to put him to the sword and fled into Egypt, did not the king send a band even into Egypt who brought out Uriah to his death? And is Jeremiah himself to live? The man must die!

And Jeremiah said, Blow the trumpets throughout the land, gather together, go into the walled cities, set up the standards; for the Lord has sent a fierce nation, a scowling people, against you—lament and howl! The king and the princes are afraid, the heart of the king shall sink and the hearts of the princes, the priests and prophets are dismayed because of the fierce anger of the Lord. Run through the streets of Jerusalem, search in its broad places for a just man, and I, said the Lord, will pardon the city. And I answered, Surely these must be the poor—they are the foolish; I will go to the great, for those know the way of the Lord, to the chambers painted in vermilion, with ceilings of cedar, smelling of incense of Sheba and the burning of sweet cane—as a cage is full of birds, so their houses of deceit; they have grown fat, the folds and collops of their faces shine. Take away the battlements; they are not Mine! says the Lord. From the least of them to the greatest they are covetous; from the priest to the prophet—every one is false. I will take from them, the Lord says, their mirth and

gladness, the voice of the bridegroom and the voice of the
bride, the sound the millstones make and the light of the
candle.

I looked about
and there was no one; all the birds of heaven were fled;
the fruitful place was a wilderness,
and the cities of Judah were broken down.
A great people, whose language you do not know, is coming
     from the north; they grasp bow and spear, their voice is
     like the sea, and they ride upon horses
to mar the pride of Judah, the great pride of Jerusalem;
we shall not go into the fields
for fear of them—
Daughter of Zion,
comely and delicate woman,
the Lord has called Zion a green olive tree;
with the crash of thunder
He has kindled a fire upon it
and the branches of it are broken.
If one goes into the fields, he sees them thick with slain;
if he enters the city, he sees those that are sick with famine.
Because of the sword, because of the famine and of the
     pestilence,
Jerusalem is given to the Chaldeans that fight against it!
At this Pash-hur shouts again, Should not men like this die?
But the elders reply, He prophesies in the name of the Lord—
     he shall not die!

76

Because of their abominations under every tree,
on every hill, let them die,
because they did not care for poor or weak,
but ate the fatted steer from out the stall,
and on their couches in the ivory houses
early in the morning were drinking wine,
let them die.

Because the lot of some was death, the lot of some, the sword,
the lot of others, famine, and of the rest, exile;
but these wept beside the waters of Babylon and Rome,
and did not forget Jerusalem nor the citadel of the Lord,
let them live, let them live.

## Joshua at Shechem
*Joshua XXIV:13*

You Hebrews are too snug in Ur,
said God; wander about waste places,
north and south leave your dead;
let kings fight against you,
and the heavens rain fire and brimstone
on you. And it was so.
And God looked again and saw
the Hebrews with their sons and daughters
rich in flocks and herds,
with jewels of silver
and jewels of gold.
And God said, Be slaves
to Pharaoh. And it was so.
And God looked again and saw
the Hebrews at the fleshpots,
with fish to eat,
cucumbers and melons.
And God said, Be gone
into the wilderness by the Red Sea
and the wilderness of Shur and the wilderness
of Shin; let Amalek come upon you,
and fiery serpents bite you. And it was so.
And God looked again and saw in a land of brooks and
    springs and fountains,
wheat and barley,
the Hebrews, in a land on which they did not labor,
in cities which they did not build,
eating of vineyards and olive trees which they did not plant.
And God scattered them—
through the cities of the Medes, beside the waters of Babylon;
they fled before Him into Egypt and went down to the sea in
    ships;
the whales swallowed them,
the birds brought word of them to the king;
the young men met them with weapons of war,
the old men with proverbs—
and God looked and saw the Hebrews
citizens of the great cities,
talking Hebrew in every language under the sun.

## Luzzato
## Padua 1727

The sentences we studied are rungs upon the ladder Jacob saw;
the law itself is nothing but the road;
I have become impatient of what the rabbis said,
and try to listen to what the angels say.
I have left Padua and am in Jerusalem at last, my friend;
for, as our God was never of wood or bone,
our land is not of stones or earth.

### 79

### Jerusalem the Golden

#### I

#### *The Lion of Judah*

The men of war spoke: Your hand against mine.
Mine against yours. The field is mine! The water is mine!
If the city is taken, kill the men of war,
kill every male; rip up the women with child!
The prophet has said, Let not their cattle live,
not even calf nor lamb before the Lord;
and Samuel, the old man, so feeble he leaned against his staff,
cried to Saul, Give me their king,
give me their smiling king to cut into pieces before the Lord.
But Nathan said to the king, even David, the great king,
You have dealt deceitfully with the Hittite, your faithful
    servant;
and you shall not build the Lord's house,
because your hands have shed much blood.

#### II

#### *The Shield of David*

Then spoke the prophets: Our God is not of clay,
to be carried in our saddle-bags;
nor to be molten of silver or fine gold,
a calf to stand in our houses with unseeing eyes, unbending
    knees;

Who is the King of Glory?
He is from everlasting to everlasting;
we go down to the darkness of the grave,
but all the lights of heaven are His.

The smoke of your sacrifices is hateful, says the Lord,
I hate your festivals, your feasts, and your fasts;
worship Me in righteousness;
worship Me in kindness to the poor and weak,
in justice to the orphan, the widow, the stranger among you,
and in justice to him who takes his hire from your hand;
for I am the God of Justice, I am the God of Righteousness.

## III

### Spinoza

He is the stars,
multitudinous as the drops of rain,
and the worm at our feet,
leaving only a blot on the stone;
except God there is nothing.

God neither hates nor loves, has neither pleasure nor pain;
were God to hate or love, He would not be God;
He is not a hero to fight our enemies,
nor like a king to be angry or pleased at us,
nor even a father to give us our daily bread, forgive us our
    trespasses;
nothing is but as He wishes,
nothing was but as He willed it;
as He wills it, so it will be.

## IV

### Karl Marx

We shall arise while the stars are still shining,
while the street-lights burn brightly in the dawn,
to begin the work we delight in,
and no one shall tell us, Go,
you must go now
to the shop or office you work in
to waste your life for your living.
There shall be no more war, no more hatred;

none of us shall die of sickness;
there shall be bread and no one hunger for bread—
and fruit better than any a wild tree grew.
Wheels of steel and pistons of steel
shall fetch us water and hew us wood;
we shall call nothing mine—nothing for ourselves only.
Proclaim to the seed of man
throughout the length and breadth of the continents,
From each according to his strength,
to each according to his need.

# VIII
# In Memoriam: 1933
# 1934

*In Memoriam: 1933* was also, like *Jerusalem the Golden*, published by the Objectivist Press in 1934. The contents were reprinted from *The Menorah Journal*. Most of the last poem and three brief extracts from the others were reprinted in the 1962 selected poems, *By the Waters of Manhattan*, with the speakers' names omitted. The present text follows the first edition, corrected at a couple of points from the 1962 printing. For details see the Appendix.

# 1. Samaria Fallen: 722 B.C.E.

*The Sentry.* Samaria is fallen, king and princes of Judah!
From the roof see now for yourselves
how hidden in fourfold wings of smoke
the Assyrian bull gores
and stamps the loveliest city of Israel
into pebbles and ashes.
    *The King.* Why do you all,
priests and captains, prophets and princes, servants, serfs and
    slaves,
delight in bringing me news
worse and still worse, as if speaking the fear of your cowardly
    hearts
were enchantment against it—
is there never a hamlet in all Israel to go up in smoke,
never a grove,
but you must hurry here to tell me Samaria itself is fallen?
    *The Sentry.* Have we not counted the cities of Israel
as a poor man counts the coins that must last him or he
    starves;
have I not notched the losses of Israel
upon my breastbone, that I am not to know when Samaria
    falls,
where Samaria burns? If it has been the guilt of my feet
to hurry here with bad news, how swiftly would they have run
to bring you cause for joy and rejoicing!
    *One of the Guard.* An Israelite is come:
he can talk as yet no more than a gasping fish,
but leans against our wall, breathing deep and quickly
the sweet air of Judah, as if he had nearly lost the trick of
    breathing.
    *The Israelite.* The mounds their captives, Israelites among
    them,
had been building higher and higher
overtopped us—
the swarm of us
who had hurried behind the stout walls, into the rooms of
    stone,
from the fields, the vineyards, and the pastures;
and they looked down upon Samaria,
as a boy coming upon a habitation of ants
leans over it—

streets and store-rooms, galleries and walls—
the little heap
sand beneath his foot and the lives of its multitude
his.
Then from our lurking places we saw a commotion
in the Assyrian camp and thought it perhaps
such as Saul had once seen among the Philistines
when Jonathan and his armor-bearer climbed among them;
and in broad daylight the Assyrians marched away,
king and captains, soldiers and captives,
and we thought,
Perhaps the Lord has interceded for us at last;
but the host marched towards Egypt,
and left only a single captain and his men to storm the city—
so little was Samaria of the marble palaces for Nineveh,
so small a mouthful Israel and his ten tribes!
The strength of the ants is their multitude,
but Israel is few
and *these* captives,
to be taken a thousand miles,
beyond the great rivers,
among the cities of the Medes, into the outermost provinces,
lost among multitudes.
As for me, what god was in me—
but as I saw troop after troop of captives,
knotted to each other with rope, whipped along,
marched off in clouds of dust,
I who was among those still untied,
sprang away through the files of bowmen,
among the wheeling chariots and prancing horses,
spears and arrows kicking up dust about me,
hearing the shouts and thinking only,
Let it be death if it must be death,
but if it is life, I am free.

   *One of the Princes.* An unlucky day it was for you, Joseph,
when your sons shouted, To your tents, Israel,
what share have we in Judah?
when you forsook the holy kingdom of the sons of David,
and, worshipping the golden calves of Jeroboam,
came no more to the temple of our God;
then, as one who goes from his city
and meets in a path a band of thieves
and his throat is cut for his cloak,

as an animal is taken for its hide;
as a child, wandering in its play
beyond the street of its father's house,
caught and trussed and shipped for a silver penny
over leagues of desert or the pathless sea—
so you are lost, Israel.
    *Another of the Princes.* Let the king command those who
        are skilled in words,
to make a lament for the tribes of Israel
that shall outlast the monuments of the Assyrians:
let them tell of the glory of Joseph in Egypt;
how Zebulun and Naphtali under Barak and Deborah
fought the kings of Canaan beside the river Kishon
until the river swept them away;
how Menasseh, Naphtali and Asher followed Gideon;
how Japhtah of Gilead fought the Ammonites,
and of Samson the Danite who fought the Philistines;
let them tell of the prophets of Israel:
of Samuel who anointed Saul of Benjamin king,
of Elijah the Tishbite who prophesied against the priests of
        Baal,
and of Hosea who pleaded with Ephraim.
The wisdom of Deborah and Hosea,
the bravery of Barak and Gideon,
the strength of Samson,
the zeal of Samuel and the saintliness of Elijah
are gone from us to be lost among the cities of the Medes;
Israel and Judah were small among the nations,
small and afraid, but they were brothers,
quarreling and striking at each other,
and holding each other by the hand;
now Israel, the stronger,
whose land was fertile and whose cities numerous,
whose tribes were ten and ours are only two—
lament for Israel, poets of Judah,
as David lamented for his brother Jonathan.
    *The King.* Let those of you who are magicians and sorcerers
whisper your incantations and answer me;
answer me, you who are priests
and sacrifice the doves, the lambs and rams of our people
upon the altars of our God,
bright with undying fires of perfumed wood;
answer, you who are learned in the wisdom of Egypt,

and you who are wise with the learning of the Chaldeans;
you prophets and you sons of prophets, answer me;
answer, you who are skilled in war,
who are captains of my bands,
tell me what Judah and Jerusalem are to do,
what I am to do now, the anointed of the Lord,
the son of David,
before the Assyrians shout their taunts at our walls
and at our God,
while their captives are building the siege-works above our
    towers.

   *The Chief of the Captains.* It is an old saying of our people
that the battle is not always to the strong;
were it otherwise there would be no beasts but the young lions,
no birds but eagles, no fish but Leviathan—
God has given each his life and his strength.
If the Assyrian, like the very locusts for number,
come against us, his horses and his chariots
will ride us down,
and he will take our fenced cities, even Jerusalem.
Now I say to the king, Let us choose men,
even as Gideon when he fought the Midianites
and took the gold moons of their camels,
and make ourselves places in the hills,
even as David on the rocks of En-gedi,
as Moses when he fled into the desert,
where no riders can follow and no chariot come;
if the citizens live, what matter that the cities are broken down.
Let the weak die, but the hardy need not fear;
in our strongholds we shall outstay the Assyrians
until, as a wind blows and is still,
their empire is like that of Egypt now,
as the might of the Philistines;
for if the righteous die, so do the wicked;
if death is a tyrant, he also frees.
We must become what we were—soldiers,
no longer watching herds for others to harry,
gathering the summer fruits for others to rob.

   *A Prince.* Your captain, my lord, has spoken like a soldier,
and cautiously, as a captain should;
but, before a siege, I have heard the herald's speech,
and, I think, we need not fight at the citadel
before the walls are lost.

Because on the hills and in caves,
as our father Jacob became Israel,
we shall become Esaus,
rather than to give up cities and fields,
our vineyards and our olive trees,
let us pay his tribute to the Assyrian.
Let us cut the gold from the pillars of the temple
and take the cups and basins from its treasury,
the candlesticks and shields of gold, of silver, and of brass,
and send them as a present to the Assyrian;
for it is better that we lose this than all,
or even that we lose all than our lives.

    *The Prophet.* The strength of soldiers, the skill of the captain,
and the wisdom of councillors, cannot save us;
neither arms nor craft will save us
from the multitude of Assyria or the multitudes of Egypt;
the Lord our God alone can save us.
Who is the Lord our God? The God of Righteousness.
The God of Justice will not let the just perish utterly;
the God of Judah hates the wrongdoer:
though he seem to touch the stars with the plume of his helmet,
he shall leave no footprint on the rock
and the wind of morning
shall sweep his tracks from the sand.
Even though your grey hairs go bloody to the grave,
and the chariots press their ruts
across the bodies of your children in the dust,
fear not, you who believe in the Lord:
whether a remnant is hidden in the caves of Judah
or are slaves in the cities of those who speak a language
    unknown to you,
so long as Jacob remembers his God,
and binds the ordinances of the Lord upon his hand and brow,
hammers them upon the doorpost,
and thinks of them when he rises to work and when he lies
    down to rest,
Jerusalem is not taken, nor has Judah perished,
neither has the God of Judah become like the idol of a captured
    city,
that lies, blackened with smoke and blood, fallen from his
    throne.

## 2. Babylon: 539 B.C.E.

*An Elder.* Our fathers were saved from the deaths
others died by hunger, plague, or sword,
when the cities of Judah and Jerusalem itself were taken,
and from the deaths so many died
along the journey that left our fathers
—the hills of Judah and the sea
out of sight many months and years—
exiles by the quiet waters and willows of Babylon;
but for us the noise of battle, not the battle itself,
is over; there is no shouting of soldiers
to warn us; no arrows; no shrieks
of the wounded;
only the suction
of this city
to pull us off our feet
until the remnant of Judah—Jerusalem and our God forgotten—
are particles in the dust of Babylon,
like other thousands and tens of thousands
Babylon has taken.
    *Another Elder.* Did the Lord, whom our fathers served,
come from the sky to stand beside them,
or even from the safety of the clouds with His lightnings
save His citadel?—
an aloof God, saving a few alive
of all Judah's thousands and tens of thousands.
Is there another people who, their cities taken,
the temple of their God become the stones it had been,
and they themselves scattered from the land,
are still worshippers of its God?
Nor, as it might have happened, are we captives among a
    savage people,
a brutish people, living in tents or caves:
these Babylonians are a great people,
living in palaces and gardens—
but we were only shepherds and herdsmen,
tenders of vineyards and of trees, ploughmen;
this is a nation of merchants and warriors,
priests of triumphant gods.
It was meant for ill to us,
but it has been for good, as to Joseph
who was brought to Egypt among slaves

to be second in his master's and in the king's house.
   *Messenger.* To all you Jews,
captives of Babylon,
Cyrus the Persian, worshipper of one god and hater of idols,
proclaims,
Joy and rejoicing!
Your enemy is about to fall
and Babylon become a proverb among the nations!
Return to Judah,
rebuild Jerusalem
and the temple of your God;
your captivity is ended!
   *The First Elder.* Surely the sun rises in the east!
Let it not be said that God has forgotten Judah,
or that the Lord was aloof
when puddles of blood stood in the streets of Jerusalem;
we looked for one of us—
and our deliverer is a stranger;
now let us hear no more of the God of Judah,
but tell us of the Lord of the Universe and of Eternity,
before whom the multitudes of Babylonia
are as powerless
as when their cities,
the great angels of granite before their palaces,
the great gods and the lesser gods,
will be looked for with spoons in the desert
and remembered
only because Judah has remembered them for evil.
   *An Elder.* It was hard for our fathers when they were slaves
     in Egypt,
building a mountain range of granite
along the flat banks of the Nile,
under the quick fists and staffs of taskmasters,
to leave the pots of fish that were theirs for the taking
and the plentiful sweet water
for the wilderness
and the knives of its tribes;
how much harder will it be for you, Judah,
to leave the gardens of Babylon,
the suits of linen and the cloaks of wool,
the meats and the cool fruits and wine
to become again dusty shepherds and herdsmen
on your barren hills, Judah;

to toil in your fields
eating only of what they shall plant,
if locusts and grasshoppers
leave what is saved from drouth and the storm,
and thieves and armed bands
what is spared by the locusts and worms.
Now shall the longings of your heart
and the words of your mouth, Jacob,
the sighs and groans, the cries and outcries of fifty years,
be put to the proof;
for the time is come of choosing and refusing:
your deliverer
calls upon Judah with the crash of thunder,
speaking your name with the voice of the earthquake.
 *The Prince of the Captivity.* Servant of Cyrus,
who hates even as we do,
the vanity of idols,
in a world where their worshippers are like the sands for
      number,
those who love the truth are drawn to each other
like particles of iron that have known the loadstone;
build on each other like coral in the sea
against the waves, the tides and spring tides, tempests and
      typhoons,
that would sweep us all away!
The Jews are few; Judah is small among the nations,
without cities and land,
and you Persians have become a mighty people;
but in the battle we have known a pebble in a sling
to do as much
as a spear weighing many shekels of brass,
and Judah will not forget the friendliness of Cyrus.
Now let the young men who are ill at ease
where all the ground is field and garden, street and square,
and all the water is canals,
or the smooth river flowing between steps,
men who like the taste of salt better than that of honey,
try their strength against the hills
and from the rubbish heaps that are Jerusalem
rebuild the city;
replant the land
with olive trees and fig trees, with vineyards and fields of
      barley, fields of wheat;

so shall Judah like a tree that has seen many tribes—
many cities become mounds and heaps—
flourish and renew itself;
for here we are only so much timber,
although smoothed and polished.
And there is other work to do in Babylon—
in courtyards, where flowers and leaves are brilliant
against a white-washed wall, the only noise
that of the fountain and the long leaves of the palms;
in cool rooms
where one need only put out his hand
to take food from the dish
or lift the cup to his lips
while the noise of the street
touches the listener no more than rain;
here others have their work,
like the stars in their orbits, seemingly
motionless,
but shining, not without influence,
upon the action of the world.
Let hands build the walls
hands more numerous
may pull down again,
but we must build in Babylon
another Zion
of precepts, laws, ordinances and commandments
to outlast stone or metal,
between every Jew and the fury or blandishment of any land—
that shall keep up a man as much as bread
and swallows of water in his belly, strengthen him
like links of armor on his body.
Let other people come as streams
that overflow a valley
and leave dead bodies, uprooted trees and fields of sand;
we Jews are as the dew,
on every blade of grass,
trodden under foot today
and here tomorrow morning.

## 3. The Academy at Jamnia: *Anno 70*

*A Rabbi.* When I was a boy, sent a captive to Rome,
the ship was dashed, stern foremost, upon a rock,
and other rocks, smooth with weeds, across which the waves
    were sliding,
stretched beyond, as far as we could see;
when I heard the crash
and saw the steep deck sloping
to the dark water, into which Romans and slaves were spilled,
their hands and feet
finding no hold or step,
and no cry from all those mouths
sound
in the howling wind,
yet there was no such terror in my heart
as now.
    *Another Rabbi.* In the Galilean hills,
a troop of Romans and Idumeans hunting us,
I hid in a cave
that led I knew not where, but knew it safe,
for the mouth was low,
in a thicket and covered well with vines,
known only to our band and the serpents;
and there was an earthquake—
so slight a shock that, seated as I was,
it rocked me gently,
but enough to start
the ledge
under which we crept
crashing,
and I in the dusty blackness
bruising my hands against the rock
where the twilight of the opening
had been shining.
To stay there was to die;
through vents
I could not stand in,
too low
for walking
and at last
for crawling,
vaults so large,

I hardly heard the
waterfall,
upon a shore
without wave or ripple,
leaning away from
chasms—
cliff below cliff,
down which the falling
stone would strike and
fall, strike
ever fainter,
until it fell in silence,
my hands, antennae,
around stalagmites and rocks, through dung
of bats, touching
cold rock, cold flesh of shuddering
things, bats flying
against my face, squeezing
their mouselike faces
between my lips—
now
to stay here is to die.
   *Johanan.* Times like these
may strengthen us, as water becomes steam
and climbs to the clouds, or ice
and for a time iron;
our anger at the legions
that camp about Jerusalem,
sure of their eagles that have flown
at a thousand victories,
until the world is become only the suburbs
of their city
and the idols
sergeants of their emperor;
the stench from our heaps of slain
in the fields about the city
and from those that lie
singly in the gutters,
dead of hunger or the plague or a stray arrow,
heat our bodies
to swiftness
and strength muscles never had,
freeze our breasts

hard as breastplates,
and our hands
as their blades;
and yet,
as our quarreling captains know,
and those schismatics who stab each other—
Jerusalem will fall,
this month or next,
this year or this decade,
and Vespasian or his son
and the meanest follower
walk, smiling at the bronze signs
that forbid the foreigner, into the temple,
looking about in the
empty gloom for the
God who has escaped them,
even into the holy of holies,
where only the high priest goes
only on the holiest day.
Here we are
like a pool that the rains have left
in a hollow of the street,
drying slowly in the shade,
and every day it lasts, it stinks the more.
    *Another Rabbi.* Saul, never doubting Samuel,
knew that he would die on Mount Gilboa
in the morning,
he and Jonathan,
yet they went into battle;
and we, knowing Jerusalem is lost,
our temple to be open not only to Romans and Idumeans,
Greeks and Syrians, but the dogs of the street
will run about its stones,
the birds of the ditches nest there,
and the glory of Judah
darken as a stream darkens at twilight,
may well do no less than Saul and Jonathan.
    *Johanan.* You have seen a bush beside the road
whose leaves the passing beasts pluck at
and whose twigs are sometimes broken
by a wheel, and yet it flourishes,
because the roots are sound—
such a heavy wheel is Rome;

these Romans,
all the legions of the East
from Egypt and Syria,
the islands of the sea and the rivers of Parthia,
gathered here
to trample down Jerusalem,
when they have become a legend
and Rome a fable,
that old men will tell of in the city's gate,
the tellers will be Jews and their speech Hebrew.
The hurricane, leaving its dead or dying,
leaves also the healing and the hale,
but the sunshine and the stars,
the air we breathe,
the daily bread,
the words we listen to,
and the thoughts of our hearts
become ourselves and our sons.
We who have outlived the empires
of the ancients—Egypt, Assyria, and Babylon,
withstood their conquests or been conquered
and, captives or fugitives, slaves or strangers,
still were Jews,
have nothing to fear from Rome;
I fear
the teachings of the stranger
and the renegade:
it was not because of the captains of Assyria
but because of the priests of Baal
that the ten tribes were lost among the Medes.
Now, instead of the calves
of the rustic Canaanites,
the gods of Olympus—
Aphrodite and Artemis, Zeus and Apollo:
gods of those
who have slaves
and spend their days in gymnasiums,
or in groves talking of wisdom,
and their nights at banquets—
Sodomites;
but our God is the God of Adam,
who must earn his bread,
and yet not the God of the fishermen,

of slaves
and the silly women of Rome,
the followers of Jesus,
who have scraps of the psalms
and the teachings of the Essenes
and of Hillel,
who talk of love and hell-fire,
who are witty about the Torah but believe
in a God who has a Son,
in the Virgin who gives birth,
and the God Who is slain and rises from the dead.
Jerusalem will sink and we must
escape the whirlpool
of its sinking
and save, not ourselves—
its books
in the cupboards of our minds—
but the city
of which these streets and walls,
even citadel and temple,
are only body;
if Judah
shall ride the flood
which rolls down upon the world
to bring all living under its cold waters,
come,
brothers in learning as in arms,
when battlements and fortresses,
strongholds and castles sink,
only a school
will float our cargo.

## 4. The Synagogue Defeated: *Anno* 1096

*The Monk.* A thousand, yes, more than a thousand, years
    ago
God sent His only Son
to bring peace on earth,
good will to all mankind,
and the Jews took Him
and bound Him
and brought Him before the governor of their land
shouting that He called Himself the Messiah,
that is, their king,
and they scourged the Christ
and put a crown of thorns upon His head
and crucified Him,
as daily they crucify Him still
by their malice towards all Christians
and by their usury which holds in bondage
the bravest.
Many of you have often thought, no doubt,
your fingers itching
for the hilt of your sword or closing tightly
upon your staff, if only you were there
when they led the Lord
through the streets of Jerusalem
or when they nailed Him
to the cross,
how you would have burst through the crowds
to stand beside Him
and have a thrust at that circle of dark faces,
those jeering mouths.
The glory of such a death,
the bliss of it,
were you only there in the muck,
trampled upon by the Jews,
even if no cherubim and seraphim,
angels and archangels
were streaming through the firmament
to greet you,
shouting hosannahs
and singing psalms of praise!
No,
I think you would have denied Him,

as Peter did;
even as He was hanging by His bleeding hands,
you would have denied Him twice or thrice
to the maidservants and the grooms,
before the cocks had crowed;
for is there a town of yours
in which there is not a Jew's stone house,
while many and many a Christian is glad of a hut,
a street along which Jews do not walk, yes, ride,
jingling their spurs,
and none, for all your paternosters, orisons, and masses,
lifts his hand,
and only a child, perhaps,
throws a stone at them
or calls out an unfriendly word.
But your knights
speak softly and pledge them the land of God
for the devil's little coins;
yes, many acres are now in the Jews' chests,
while they go up and down
unashamed before the crucifixes,
sowing a little heresy here,
a little blasphemy there—
brothers in Christ, shall it be said
that the Jew's stone walls and oak door
are stronger than the hands of Christians?
If oak is stronger than flame
and iron than fire,
and a cluster of toadstools
than the step of a man!
Burn and blaze,
step and stamp;
the Jews and their parchments
to the flames,
their children to the font!
   *The Painter:* Priests and monks
and the preaching friars
may mouth as much as they like
in Latin, or your language,
of Jesus
talking to the fishermen
as they pull in the nets
full of dark seaweed and shining fish;

the blood trickling down His face
in twenty little streams
from the crown of thorns,
and His fingers twisted
about the spikes driven through His hands;
or the ranks of saints
moving before Him in Heaven
as the waves of a stream in sunlight—
you understand their speech because we paint it
on the white-washed walls of churches;
hating whatever is ugly,
preachers,
we paint the knights with lean faces
and smooth yellow hair,
sunburnt and windburnt,
who are not afraid to kill or die for lord or lady,
and the ladies with hollow cheeks,
bodies big with child,
who look proudly out of grey eyes
and give to beggars
with a sidelong glance;
the healing trees
in flower beside the street,
sending their petals to drift upon the stones;
the night
bringing man and beast
smarting in the glare and sweat of day
darkness—
quiet fields and streets;
the day itself
beating with innumerable rays
the night into shadows
and shaping out of chaos
the loveliness
of lifeless and of living things,
washing their colors clean of darkness.
In a field,
feeling the sunshine
as if your flesh were glass—
twigs and leaves in order
on every bush and tree,
bright flowers below,
bright birds about and above—

should you see
the fat body of a snake
and the flat head lifted, eyes watching,
would you not spring away
to catch up a stick and stones;
or, along a road
at dead of night,
toads thumping
about your feet,
would you not step upon the lumps
but for disgust?
The hairy insects
on your table,
the Jews—
brush to the floor
and stamp into the rushes!
The leaves of your city are become
green skeletons
from which hang worms and the white threads
of worms; citizens,
like the rain for number,
splash and dash
against walls and cobblestones—
wash away the Jews!
Set the beauty of flames
to their ugliness;
pick and pluck,
rake and sweep,
kindle;
let not the hair
of a Jew's beard
escape in the wind!
    *The Crowd.* The burgomaster!
    *The Burgomaster.* I know you—
shoemakers, makers of hoods or jerkins,
herdsmen, shepherds, and farmers,
merchants of cheese and wool,
priests and soldiers;
so were your fathers,
so your sons,
by sunlight and starlight in our places—
in fields and streets,
in houses, church or castle,

with love and charity
to those below us, in obedience and love
to those above,
from sacrament to sacrament,
from baptism to extreme unction.
But what are you in the city,
one of the synagogue?
A Jew,
come from the east or west,
and going north or south;
no trade but buyer and seller,
no merchandise but money;
every man's servant
and the liege of none;
pulling off his cap to the peasants
and saying, my lords, but in his heart calling the lords louts.
We have no need of you
and no place for you;
we did not bid you come
and will not let you go—
what you have gathered
here and in all Christendom
shall be the harvest
your blood shall grow for us
between the cobblestones of our streets.

## 5. Spain: *Anno* 1492

*Torquemada.* Now that Castile and Aragon in holy wedlock
are Spain,
and the last city of the Moors in Spain is Spanish
except for Moor and Jew—
about every crucifix in every market-place
and in the court itself the Jews!—
as seven centuries of Christian valor, Christian piety
triumph
stay not your hand;
Spain of the knights,
one in fealty to your majesties,
become one in faith,
Spain of the saints!
Like the sun,
rising as our Savior from His tomb into the brilliant sky
blaze
until the clouds that still obscure the light
are drawn into His brightness
and earth is brilliant as the sky is bright.
Spain newly united
still divided—
as the season of cold is the season of darkness
in the spring of our rejoicing that the Moor is gone from Spain,
the Jew go too!
But if the Spaniard speaks,
I speak no less a Christian:
throw away the curse, you Jews,
of fifteen hundred years;
stay and prosper
and Church and Heaven prosper,
in our nets a goodly catch.
Think not that we want aught of you
but your souls;
your money and your jewels—
all your trash—
keep if you stay and are Christian,
take if you are Jews and go;
we ask of you nothing but your Judaism
which has brought you so much misery
and will bring each of you—
the youngest and the gentlest—

to the flames of Hell
and the worm that dies not.
We give you,
miserable sinners,
the waters of
Paradise;
we give you the blessings of the saints,
the blessings of Mary, the blessed mother of Christ,
and the blessings of our Lord Jesus.
 *Isabella.* There is a sweet reasonableness in the words of our
  prior;
it is Saint Dominic who speaks to us
through his Dominican or Saint James himself.
 *Abrabanel.* No noble in your court, your majesties,
proud of his forefather, conquering Goth or Visigoth or Vandal,
is of an older Spanish line than we—
Jews in Iberia before the Romans came.
No noble boasting his service
boasts of more than that Jew who through a thousand shoals
  and reefs
piloted Aragon to Castile—your marriage and Spain's glory.
The rest of us, many tens of thousands,
serve you humbly
in smithy, field or vineyard, soldiers or physicians,
as we have served in Spain two thousand years,
Spaniards, true to your majesties
as we are to the God of Israel—and of Spain,
unlike the others only in our faith
for which, if we must answer,
we shall answer to our God.
 *Torquemada.* Since all we do,
and each word spoken, if only in our hearts,
must be in worship—
not a leaf falls slowly but in His service—
to be unlike us in our faith
is to be unlike in everything.
True, you Jews must answer to your God,
and in the flames and burning ice of Hell forever
you shall answer;
but we too, priests, bishops, queen and king,
must answer for you:
farmer or captain answers;
shall we be less answerable for souls?

*Abrabanel.* You do not honor your God
by bringing Him captives,
like a mere emperor
who must have retainers and retinue,
serfs and forced labor;
the loadstone
without visible motion
draws to itself every particle of iron;
the sword—even though a winged angel swings it—
served only
to drive Adam from his paradise.
Your fingers stiff with rings and jewels,
you dishonor your faith, your majesties, by cruelty,
give it whatever noble name you will
as princes make a rogue knight or lord.
Will thieves and pirates be gentler with us
than your constables and soldiers?—
your majesties will hear of many
ripped up for the jewels it will be said they swallowed;
many left by sailors to die on reefs and sandbars
for a smock or a pair of hose; many dead of plague
or found like birds in winter
dead in the fields about towns or like fish upon a beach;
many will die as slaves at work
beasts would be fitter for but costlier,
who have written a page of Castilian
or handled a Toledo blade with the best.
And yet the weak has each his strength,
Spain of Spaniard, Basque, and Catalonian, Moor and Gypsy,
else all beasts were tigers,
all fish sharks,
and only giants left;
the stricken remember—
as wounds and scars last longer than the blow—
and if drops of water wear channels in the rock
on which the earth itself is,
in the action of centuries
how powerful are tears.
Would you have our religion
like our clothes—for comfort and the eyes of men,
put off at night,
and we left lying naked in the darkness?
The body is like roots stretching down into the earth—

forcing still a way over stones and under rock, through sand,
sucking nourishment in darkness,
bearing the tread of man and beast,
and of the earth forever;
but the spirit—
twigs and leaves
spreading
through sunshine
or the luminous darkness
of twilight, evening, night, and dawn,
moving
in every wind of heaven
and turning
to whatever corner of the sky is brightest,
compelled by nothing stronger than the light;
the body is like earth,
the spirit like water
without which earth is sand
and which must be free or stagnant;
or if the body is as water,
the spirit is like air
that must have doors and windows
or else is stuffy and unbreathable—
or like the fire
of which sun and stars have been compounded,
which Joshua could command but for an hour.
    *Isabella.* If our eye offends us,
pluck it out!
Even so, we will sweep away the Jews
from every town and hamlet, field and corner of our dominion,
though they are the sands for number.
Go and begone—but stay as Christians;
come and be dear to us,
as the Prodigal!
    *Abrabanel.* We Jews have been accused of love of wealth,
but not for all our wealth in Spain,
fields and vineyards, houses of timber and houses of stone
that we must leave,
and all the wealth that will be stolen from us,
will we stay;
we Jews have been accused of arrogance,
but not for all the dignities that we must leave,
our offices and honors

in this, the proudest court of Christendom,
will we stay;
we Jews have been accused of love of life,
delighting in the flesh,
but though we shall die along a thousand roads
we will not stay—
striking roots
somewhere
to flourish
as we flourished,
giving shade and fruit.

## 6. Poland: *Anno* 1700

*An Old Jew.* There we were throughout Poland,
a Jew or two in each hamlet, a dozen in each village,
and a thousand or so in every town—
who knows how many thousands and tens of thousands—
going about in the dust of summer
or against the cold wind with noses deep in our collars,
hands pushed into our sleeves,
selling and buying—
this lord's cow and that lord's sack of wheat,
scheming as hard to earn our bread
as a minister might to rule a kingdom,
when, crash!
as a dish slips from a woman's hands
and lies in pieces on the ground,
our bustling ended,
and we were scurrying from the Cossacks
straight for the towns—
their bands trotting along the roads,
booty hanging about their saddles,
lances tall as the chimneys;
many a Jew and Pole were skewered together
on those lances, or hanged
side by side with a pig between them—
boughs were heavy with that harvest;
and still the Cossacks came
breeding in the plunder,
until cannon no longer stopped them,
and gates of towns could not keep them out—
Kiev was taken;
the dead along highway and byway,
pools of blood in streets and houses
drew the troops of them on their swift horses out of the steppes,
many and as pitiless as insects.
　　*A Young Jew.* How tiresome these old stories are—
Assyrians and Syrians,
now Germans and now the Cossacks;
how the Cossacks plundered and killed the Jews of Poland
or that the glory of the Jews in Spain
was muddied
as sunshine on a pool by cattle.
Tell us of the Jews along the Rhine

before the crusades; before the Inquisition,
upon the plains from which the snowy Pyrenees are seen;
tell us of our glory in Babylon,
of our glory in Egypt,
that we who in the alleys and the byways
of these Polish cities
have only synagogues of wood,
who in the fairs and market-places sweat or freeze beside our
    booths and wagons
from dawn to darkness,
may hide that splendor
in our hearts.
    *The Old Jew.* As soldiers in their drill
charge and beat back the charge
of a foe they may never meet,
so we strengthen ourselves
in struggling with our fathers' foes, long harmless
and merely the people of our thoughts—
but some day ready again to act in flesh and blood,
surely as a hard winter brings the wolves howling
along the forest roads and even to the streets.
    *Another Jew.* These are the pools
where the market-place is sunken,
but the ground is wet
and the rain is falling everywhere.
The wind is blowing in every street—
only banging a shutter
or whirling up dust
in a corner;
but it will blow a storm again.
Unravel this world
with your nervous fingers
and reweave the knotted thread
on the loom of the Talmud;
sort the dirty rags of the world,
buyers of old clothes, ragpickers;
gather the bits
and refine it in the fire of the Torah,
buyers of bottles and rusty metal,
dealers in junk;
peddlers and keepers of stands and booths,
and even you who have stores on streets,
you great merchants who buy flax in Russia

and ship furs to Germany,
I have heard it said there is no goods like the Talmud,
no goods like the Torah.
The sun was heavy on my head,
the earth was hot beneath my shoes
in the alley
that led to other alleys
and other alleys,
but I stepped into the garden,
into the cool palace of the Torah.

    *A Young Jew.* You look at the world through printed pages—
dirty panes of glass;
and even if the pages are the Talmud
and those who have written wrote with diamonds,
the more they scratched, less clearly we can see.
I see neither rag nor bark,
flesh nor leaf,
I feel neither sticks nor stones,
cloth nor pillow,
neither rain nor snow nor wind nor sunshine;
I see God only and my spirit brightens
like a mirror;
I touch Him touching all I touch;
on earth I am as close to Him as those in Heaven.
Could I teach myself to want nothing,
nothing could be taken from me;
I should be unafraid of today or tomorrow,
and live in eternity like God.
Cold and hunger, pain and grief
do not last,
are mortal like myself;
only the joy in God has no end—
this it is that in the wind
showers the petals upon the grass,
whirls up the glistening snow,
or sweeps the dust along the streets before the storm;
it shines into me
as the sun upon a tree in winter
after rain.
Light becomes colors,
colors
light and shadows—
dusk and dawn;

tasting God in the salt water
and the sweet rain,
I sink and my feet have nothing to rest on,
I rise and my hands find nothing to hold,
and am carried slowly,
now swiftly,
towards night and towards noon.

## 7. Russia: *Anno* 1905

*A Young Jew.* The weed of their hatred
which has grown so tall
now turns towards us
many heads,
many pointed petals and leaves;
what did they whisper to each other before the ikons,
and smile at over the glasses of vodka,
the spies and gendarmes, Cossacks and police,
that a crowd of ragged strangers burst into the street
leaving crooked shields of David in every pane of glass
and a Jew here and there in the gutter
clubbed to death for his coat like an animal for its skin,
the open mouth toothless, the beard stiffened with blood—
away, Jew, away!
obey the ancient summons, hurry out of this land!

Republic,
garrisoned by the waves;
every man welcome if distressed by lord or king;
and learning free to all as the streets and highways,
free as the light of street lamps,
piped into every house as the sweet water;
nation whose founders were not leaders of legions or regiments,
or masters of the long ships of war, of bowmen or artillery,
but farmers, who spoke of liberty and justice for all
and planted these abstractions in the soil
to send their seed
by every current of wind and water
to the despotisms of the earth;
your name
is like the cool wind
in a summer day
under the tyranny of the sun;
like a warm room
when, against the tyranny of the wind,
one has come a long way
on frozen ruts and clods;
the oblongs of your buildings in the west—
smooth brightness of electric light
on the white stone
and the motorcars gliding along your crowded streets—
are as the triangles of Egypt were,

and the semicircles of the arches of Rome;
how great you have become, United States!

Or to the land of rock and sand, mountain and marsh,
where the sun still woos Delilah
and the night entraps Samson,
Palestine—
and your speech shall be Hebrew;
what the mother has spun,
the daughter shall weave;
where the father has cleared away the stones,
the son shall sow and reap;
and lives will not burn singly
in single candlesticks—
how much better to live
where his fathers have lived,
than to be going about from land to land—
wasting one's life in beginnings;
how pleasant it is
for the body to sweat in the sun,
to be cool in the wind,
from dawn until twilight,
starlight to starlight;
how much better to live in the tip of the flame,
the blue blaze of sunshine,
than creep about in corners,
safe in cracks—
dribble away your days in pennies.
In that air
salty with the deeds of heroes and the speech of prophets,
as when one has left the streets and come to the
plunging and orderly sea, the green water
tumbling into yellow sand and rushing foam,
and rising in incessant waves—
upon your hills, Judah,
in your streets and narrow places
upon your cobblestones, Jerusalem!

Yet like the worm in horseradish
for whom there is no sweeter root,
should I, setting my wits against this icy circumstance,
make, like the Eskimo, my home of it?
The dust of this Russia,

breathed these many years,
is stored in my bones,
stains the skull and cortex of my brain—
the chameleon in us
that willy-nilly
takes the color where we lie.
Should I, like Abraham, become the Hebrew,
leave Ur of the Chaldees, the accident of place,
and go to other pastures, from well to well;
or, the Jew, stay,
others buzzing on the windowpanes of heaven,
flatten myself
against the ground
at the sound of a boot;
as others choose the thistle or the edelweiss,
take the reed, knowing that the grey hairs of murderers
sometimes go bloody to the grave,
that the wicked die even as the good.
Or, a Russian,
the heat by day, the same frost at night,
the same enemies in microbes and in stars,
say,
These are my people,
Russian and Ukrainian, Cossack and Tartar, my brothers—
even Ishmael and Esau;
know myself a stitch, a nail, a word
printed in its place, a bulb screwed in its socket,
alight by the same current as the others
in the letters of this sign—*Russia.*
Or better still,
there is no Russia;
there are no peoples, only man!

Stay or go;
be still the shining piston
moving heavy wheels;
the propeller
before whom ocean and the heavens divide:
the steamer seen from the land
moves slowly
but leaves a tide
that washes shore and banks;
the airplane from the ground—
an insect crawling
but filling all the heavens with its drone;

a small cloud
raining its sound
from the wide sky.

# IX
# Separate Way
# 1936

*Separate Way* was published by the Objectivist Press in 1936. Acknowledgement was offered to "the editors of *Jewish Frontier* and *The Menorah Journal* for permission to reprint whatever they have used." The poems were titled but not numbered consecutively, as they are here following the example of the selections printed in the 1962 volume, *By the Waters of Manhattan,* which also made a few other small revisions. For details see the Appendix.

# 1

## Heart and Clock

### I

Now the sky begins to turn upon its hub—
the sun; each leaf revolves upon its stem;

now the plague of watches and of clocks nicks away
the day—
ten thousand thousand steps
tread upon the dawn;
ten thousand wheels
cross and criss-cross the day
and leave their ruts across its brightness;

the clocks
drip
in every room—
our lives are leaking from the places,
and the day's brightness dwindles into stars.

### II

If my days were like the ants,
I might carry away this mountain;
therefore, you must be precious to me,
seconds;
let them step and stamp upon you as they can,
I shall escape with a few grains.

### III

#### Evening

The dark green leaves
of grass, bushes, and trees—
the jays are hushed,
I see no squirrel scamper;
but the street lamps along the winding path
burn brightly—
the work of man is not yet over.

IV

How pleasant
the silence of a holiday
to those who listen
to the long dialogue of heart and clock.

2

Malicious women greet you saying, So this is Marie!
She was such a beautiful girl, my dears!
And afterwards you study your glass for wrinkles and hair
    graying,
as if the face of a Greek goddess were less beautiful
because its paint has been washed away a thousand years;
your beauty is like that of a tree whose beauty outlasts the
    flowers,
like that of a light constantly
losing its rays through the hours
and seasons, and still aglow
through twilight and darkness, through moths and snow.

3

I

I will write songs against you,
enemies of my people; I will pelt you
with the winged seeds of the dandelion;
I will marshal against you
the fireflies of the dusk.

II

I eat and am happy;
I am hungry—and sad;
that so little means so much
means that among the little
I am such.

## 4

## Epitaphs

### I

Drowning
I felt for a moment reaching towards me
finger tips against mine.

### II

You mice,
that ate the crumbs of my freedom,
lo!

### III

The clock strikes:
these are the steps of our departure.

### IV

A brown oak leaf
scraping the sidewalk
frightened me.

### V

Proserpine
swallowed only six seeds
of the pomegranate
and had to stay six months among the dead—
I was a glutton.

## 5

## Walking and Watching

### I

### *Summer Evening*

The black sloop at anchor
has a light in the rigging;
the waters of the river
twinkle;
the stars spring up
on the smooth twilight;

row after row,
the street lamps burst into light.

The branches,
sloping towards each other,
sway in the wind;
the leaves quiver
in the rain;
flashing when the lightning flashes,
drops of rain
become falling sparks.

III

*Desert*

The swift river, foaming into waves,
waves bursting into foam,
mile after mile,
under a windless and unclouded sky;
not a beast or bird,
neither tree nor bush, no weed or grass:
a plain of white sand
on which are scattered
black stones and boulders,
or ledge on ledge
rising in barren cliffs.

IV

The water is freezing in straight lines across the ripples;
the ice is so thin the brown leaves
are seen moving along underneath;
the wheels of the automobiles hiss
on the wet pavement;
the bridge has become only a few lines in pencil
on the grey sky—
even lines made by rule and compass.

The street curves in and out, up and down
in great waves of asphalt;
at night the granite tomb is noisy with starlings
like the creaking of many axles;
only the tired walker knows how much there is to climb,
how the sidewalk curves into the cold wind.

## 6

### Millinery District

The clouds, piled in rows like merchandise,
become dark; lights are lit in the lofts;
the milliners, tacking bright flowers on straw shapes,
say, glancing out of the windows,
It is going to snow;
and soon they hear the snow scratching the panes. By night
it is high on the sills.
The snow fills up the footprints
in the streets, the ruts of wagons and of motor trucks.
Except for the whir of the car
brushing the tracks clear of snow,
the streets are hushed.
At closing time, the girls breathe deeply
the clean air of the streets
sweet after the smell of merchandise.

## 7

### Separate Way

Take no stock in the friendly words of friends,
for in such kindness all their kindness ends;
we go our separate ways to death.

The love of father or of mother knows
the fear of sickness, the need of food and clothes,
but otherwise—we go our separate ways to death.

Kiss after kiss of the head beside you on the cushion,
but faithful only in its fashion—
we go our separate ways to death.

If you would see the phoenix burn
and in the traffic hunt a unicorn,
well, ride the subway till your death
and hold your job till you are out of breath.
We heard your jokes, your stories, and your songs,
know of your rights and all your wrongs,
but we are busy with our own affairs.

Sorry? O yes! But after all who cares?
You think that you have something still to say?
Perhaps. But you are growing old, are growing grey.
And we are too.
We'll spare another friendly word for you;
and go our separate ways to death.

8

## Depression

So proudly she came into the subway car
all who were not reading their newspapers saw
the head high and the slow tread—
coat wrinkled and her belongings in a paper bag,
face unwashed and the grey hair uncombed;

simple soul, who so early in the morning when only the
        poorest go to work,
stood up in the subway and outshouting the noise:
"Excuse me, ladies and gentlemen, I have a baby at home who
        is sick,
and I have no money, no job;" who did not have box or cap
        to take coins—
only his hands,
and, seeing only faces turned away,
did not even go down the aisle as beggars do;

the fire had burnt through the floor:
machines and merchandise had fallen into
the great hole, this zero that had sucked away so many years
and now, seen at last, the shop itself;
the ceiling sloped until it almost touched the floor—
        a strange curve
in the lines and oblongs of his life;
drops were falling
from the naked beams of the floor above,
from the soaked plaster, still the ceiling;
drops of dirty water were falling
on his clothes and hat and on his hands;
the thoughts of business
gathered in his bosom like black water

in footsteps through a swamp;

waiting for a job, she studied the dusty table at which she sat
and the floor which had been badly swept—
the office-boy had left the corners dirty;
a mouse ran in and out under the radiator
and she drew her feet away
and her skirt about her legs, but the mouse went in and out
about its business; and she sat waiting for a job
in an unfriendly world of men and mice;

walking along the drive by twos and threes,
talking about jobs,
jobs they might get and jobs they had had,
never turning to look at the trees or the river
glistening in the sunlight or the automobiles
that went swiftly past them—
in twos and threes talking about jobs;

in the drizzle
four in a row
close to the curb
that passers-by might pass,
the squads stand
waiting for soup,
a slice of bread
and shelter—
grimy clothes
their uniform;
on a stoop
stiffly across the steps
a man
who has fainted;
each in that battalion
eyes him,
but does not move from his place,
well drilled in want.

9

Messianic

The night is warm,
the river is brimming over
with the light

of street lights and electric signs;
the wires of a star
shine in the mist;
the fine spring rain will fall
smelling of earth,
the sunshine
brighten the streets;
the sparrows will wheel about the shining twigs—
a sparrow flying into a budding tree
curves about a twig to alight on another.

How far and wide
about the upper and the lower bay,
along the rivers and beside the sea,
how close and evenly
the street lamps shine:
you shall know the forests of your fathers
among these posts,
and you their deserts
upon these miles of pavement
whose mica
glistens in the sunlight and the lamplight,
in the heat of summer or the frost of winter,
wet with rain or white with snow.
Though your tribe is the smallest and you are the least,
you shall speak, you shall drill, you shall war;
and, dying,
wheeled away so swiftly
you see the sun
no larger than the evening star,
their boots shall carry your blood—
its corpuscles
seeds
that will grow in the sandy lots,
between the cobblestones of alleys and on the pavement of
     avenues.

## 10

## The Socialists of Vienna*

The rain is falling
steadily. Two by two,
a column of policemen marches
in the twilight. (Revolution!
Against our boots
strike,
flickering tongues!)
A company of soldiers
with machine-guns,
squad by squad, turns within a square
and marches down a street. (Revolution!
We are the greyhounds—
unleash us!—
to hunt these rabbits
out of the fields. *Listen to me,*
*my two wives,*
*I have killed a man!*)
Workingmen troop down the stairs
and out into the rain;
hurrah!
Revolution! (The gentleness of the deer
will never persuade the tiger from his leap.
*Strong as a million hands,*
*what Bastille or Kremlin withstands us*
*as we march, as we march?*)
Who minds the rain now?
How bright the air is;
how warm to be alive!
No children
in the hallways;
the stores closed,
not a motor car;
except for the rain,
how quiet.
Revolution!
Hurry to the power-house;
let the water out of the

*I am indebted to Ilya Ehrenbourg's *Civil War in Austria* (*New Masses*, July 3, 1934) for information. C. R.

boilers! The wires of the lamps burn dimly,
the lights in the houses
are out. Tie the red flag to the chimney,
but do not go through the streets,
where the steel-helmets have woven nets
of barbed wire;
bring guns and machine-guns
through the sewer
to each beleaguered house;
and send couriers throughout the land.
Arise, arise, you workers!
Revolution!

Put on your helmets;
troopers, tighten the straps
under your chins;
strap on revolvers;
tighten your belts,
and mount your horses; mount!
Send bullets flying through the panes of glass—
windows, mirrors, pictures;
forward, trot!
I am Fey,
I am Prince Starhemberg;
behind me is The Empire—
the princes of Austria
and the captains of Germany,
armored tanks and armored aeroplanes,
fortresses and battleships;
before us only workingmen
unused to arms and glory!

The bones in his neck part as they hang him,
and the neck is elongated;
here is a new animal
for the zoo in which are
mermaid, centaur, sphynx, and Assyrian cherub—
the face human, like their faces,
but sorrowing for a multitude,
hands and feet dangling
out of sleeves and trousers become too short,
and the neck a giraffe's—
as the neck of one who looks away from the patch of grass at

    his feet
and feeds among clouds should be.

Tell of it you who sit in the little cafés,
drinking coffee and eating whipped cream
among the firecrackers of witticisms;
tell of it you who are free to gallop about on horseback
or to ride in automobiles, or walk in gardens,
who say, Do not speak of despondency—
or any ugliness;
"Wie herrlich leuchtet
Mir die Natur!
Wie glaenzt die Sonne,
Wie lacht die Flur!"*

Karl Marx Hof, Engels Hof,
Liebknecht Hof, Matteotti Hof—
names cut in stone to ornament a house
as much as carving of leaves or fruit,
as any bust of saint and hero;
names pealing out a holiday among the ticking of clocks!—
speak your winged words, cannon;
shell with lies, radios,
the pleasant homes—
the houses built about courtyards
in which were
the noise of trees and of fountains,
the silence of statues and of flowers;
cry out, you fascists,
Athens must perish!
Long live Sparta!

---

*How splendidly Nature is alight before me! How the sun is shining, how
the meadows laugh!—Goethe.

## 11

## New Nation*

### I

*Land of Refuge*

A mountain of white ice
standing still
in the water
here forty fathoms deep
and flowing swiftly
from the north;
grampuses and whales
going by in companies,
spouting up water in streams
(these wonders of the Lord, I, Francis Higginson,
saw on the way to Salem);
a fair morning,
and still many leagues from land,
but the air warm and spiced—
yellow flowers on the sea,
sometimes singly,
sometimes in sheets;
high trees on every hill and in every dale,
on every island,
and even on the stony cliffs;
banks of earth
on which are groves of trees,
and no undergrowth of bush or brambles;
the sandy shore overrun with vines
of melons and of grapes
which the beat and surging of the sea
overflows
(this I, Arthur Barlowe, saw);
trees of sweet-smelling wood
with rind and leaves sweet-smelling
as the bark of cinnamon and leaves of bay;
soil dark and soft,
strawberries everywhere,
hickory nuts and sassafras;

*Based on Albert Bushnell Hart's *American History Told by Contemporaries*. C. R.

here are grapes white and red,
very sweet and strong,
and plums, black and red,
and single roses, white and red and damask;
we have eaten venison with the Indians,
and drunk water with spice in it—
Indian corn, even the coarsest,
makes as pleasant a meat as rice.
(Without any show of anger
the Iroquois crunched our fingers in their mouths,
and with their teeth tore off the nails;
then hacked our fingers off, joint by joint,
with stone hatchets, or with a shell too dull
to cut the sinews;
and in the stumps of our thumbs drove up spikes
until the elbow;
but so great the help of Jesus,
with this maimed hand I, Isaac Jogues,
Jesuit and priest,
baptised an Indian among the captives,
using the raindrops on a long leaf of corn.)

Let others cry, "New lands!
where Indians shall bring
kernels of gold, wagons full of gold;
whatever spills upon the way
we shall tread carelessly,
for we shall have so much of gold—
so many pearls to sew upon our clothes;
away,
unthrifty gentlemen,
to the forests of Virginia!
There are lands
to feed all the poor of England,
trees
to build each a home;
give us but axes, shovels, and ploughshares,
and away then to America,
all you poor!"
In England a watch is set about us
and we are clapt in jails,
and Holland is a dear place,
for there they live by trading—

but we are a plain country people
whose trade is husbandry,
and we would worship God as simply as the shepherds
and Galilean fishermen,
live as plainly;
away,
dissenters,
to New England!
A great wind is blowing,
heavy rain—
thick darkness;
the sailors running here and there,
shouting at one another
to pull at this and at that rope,
and the waves pouring over the ship;
landing in the rain—
the cold rain
falling steadily;
the ground wet,
all the leaves dripping,
and the rocks running with water;
the sky is cloud on cloud
in which the brief sun barely shines,
the ground snow on snow,
the cold air
wind and blast;
we have followed our God
into this wilderness
of trees heavy with snow,
rocks seamed with ice,
that in the freezing blasts
the remnant of this remnant
kindle so bright, so lasting a fire
on this continent,
prisoners of ice and darkness everywhere
will turn and come to it
to warm their hands and hearts.

II

*Brief History*

Glaciers pushing so far and surely
thaw and withdraw;
even the deep,

while the explosion of its waves
dynamites the cliffs,
leaves new lands,
new groves and habitations
beside the glittering currents flowing quickly
into the silver waters of the sun.

Here are men who find
a comfortable bed
among the rocks,
who wrap themselves
in their coats
to sleep upon the ground
while their horse feeds in the grass beside the lake;
who catch trout in the brook
and roast them on the ashes;
eat the flesh
of bear for meat, the whie meat of turkeys
for their bread, and whose salt is brought
in an iron pot across the mountains;
who live
where two hundred acres may be had
for a calf and a wool hat;
or walk where there is no road
nor any man, except the savage.

All the bells of Boston
are tolling
a solemn peal;
the market men will take no more paper money—
hard money only;
soldiers with bare feet showing through their shoes
in the snow, the smoke of the camp-fires blowing into their
        eyes;
for food a bowl of beef soup full of burnt leaves;
no house or hut, and even the sick in tents.
The rays of your light,
like the sun's, Republic of France,
shone first in the west; the eater shall give meat,
and out of the strong sweetness—
out of the bones of the French monarchy
the honey of freedom;
the bells of Philadelphia are ringing
as if for a fire,

and the crowds,
shouting and hallooing,
fill the streets;
ring, bells, throughout the night,
let no one sleep;
ring, clash, and peal
until the log cabins and cottages of cedar shingles,
the houses of grey stone or of brick,
tremble,
and the listeners
feel in their flesh
the vibrations of your metal voices
ringing,
Proclaim liberty,
proclaim liberty throughout the land!

Wrongs,
like molecules of gas that seep into a house,
explode
in particles of fire!
A captain gallops down the street,
wheels,
and the hoof of his horse
sends the pie plates shining in the sun;
his horse stops
at what is
flowing from the battlefield,
sniffs at it, and will not cross:
this is not water—
it is blood
in a thick and ropy stream.
(The dying Negress says,
I cannot eat dry hominy:
I lived in *Massa's* house,
and used to have white bread and coffee;
and I want something sweet in my mouth.)
On the lawn the Negroes dance
and clap their hands,
So glad! so glad!
Bless the Lord for freedom!
So glad! so glad!

Do not mourn the dandelions—
that their golden heads become grey

in no time at all
and are blown about in the wind;
each season shall bring them again to the lawns;
but how long the seeds of justice
stay underground,
how much blood and ashes of precious things
to manure so rare and brief a growth.

Currents of waste
wind
along the river
between the factories—
the colonnades
and sacred groves
of chimneys;
where once the road
in ruts and ridges—lines of rails
hold to a gleaming purpose,
come wind, come rain, come winter or the night;
build storey on storey out of glass;
light electric lights,
row after row, whose shining wires
will not flicker in the wind;
let the streets sound
with the horns and hosannahs of motor cars!
Man, you need no longer
drudge at plow or oar, no longer trudge;
proclaim this liberty to all!
If bread may be as plentiful,
shall we not share it
as we share water?

## 12
### Palestine under the Romans*

The east is alight as far as Hebron.
In the room of hewn stone, the vaulted room,
the priests would hear the noise of the opening of the great
        gate of the Temple;
and the goats on the mountain would sneeze
at the smell of the incense.
Colonnades, a forum, and a basilica,

*Based on the *Mishnah* as translated by Herbert Danby.

the camping-grounds of the legions; the tents of the Arabs;
an olive tree beside the winepress or the gap in the wall,
and paths that lead towards cisterns, pits, caverns, and
    winepresses:
hilly or rocky country,
and a place over which the sea rolls during a storm.

Israel is like a bird
that a creeping weasel has wounded in the head
or a man knocked against a wall—
the cattle have trampled it but still it flutters;

if there is bone enough to make the tooth of a key,
and ink enough to write two letters of the alphabet—
the house is sold and the door but not the key;
the ship is sold, the mast, the sail, the anchor, and all the
    means for steering,
but not the packing-bags or lading.
The cord that holds the balances of dealers in fine purple
and a harlot's shift that is made like network;
the hooks of porters or a weaver's pin
and the point of the sun-dial;
oil dripping into the trough from between the pressing-stone
    and the boards of the olive-press
and lamps in synagogues, in houses of study, in dark alleys.

Put out the lamp for fear of gentiles,
for fear of thieves or of an evil spirit;
when will heart and mouth agree?
Make ready all that is needful for the dead,
and anoint it, and wash it,
bind up the chin, and hire a wailing woman
and two to play dirges on the flute.

Go with a staff and a bag and a scroll of the law,
and fear not the rush of tramping shoes, at the sound of the
    shouting!
Cut it with sickles, uproot it with spades;
if it grows into the blade, it must be hoed up;
if into the ear, it must be broken off;
if into the full corn, it must be burnt.

In the evening, until midnight, until dawn,
as soon as we can tell between blue and green,
between blue and white,
when we lie down and when we stand up,
each in his own way
(though we stop to return a greeting or greet a man
out of respect, out of fear),
bringing grapes in baskets to the winepress or figs in baskets
    to the drying-place,
trampling the grain and binding it into sheaves,
or the women spinning their yarn by moonlight,
a workingman on the top of a tree or a course of stones,
or a bridgroom on the first night,
or he whose dead lies unburied before him,
and they that bear the bier and they that relieve them—
if our faces cannot, our hearts
turn towards Jerusalem
and you, the God of our fathers,
of Abraham, Isaac, and Jacob.


## 13

### Kaddish

"Upon Israel and upon the Rabbis, and upon their disciples and upon all
the disciples of their disciples, and upon all who engage in the study of the
Torah in this place and in every place, unto them and unto you be abundant
peace, grace, lovingkindness, mercy, long life, ample sustenance and
salvation, from their Father who is in Heaven. And say ye Amen." *Kaddish
de Rabbanan*, translated by R. Travers Herford.


Upon Israel and upon the rabbis
and upon the disciples and upon all the disciples of their
    disciples
and upon all who study the Torah in this place and in every
    place,
to them and to you
peace;

upon Israel and upon all who meet with unfriendly glances,
    sticks and stones and names—
on posters, in newspapers, or in books to last,
chalked on asphalt or in acid on glass,
shouted from a thousand thousand windows by radio;

who are pushed out of class-rooms and rushing trains,
whom the hundred hands of a mob strike,
and whom jailers strike with bunches of keys, with revolver
    butts;
to them and to you
in this place and in every place
safety;

upon Israel and upon all who live
as the sparrows of the streets
under the cornices of the houses of others,
and as rabbits
in the fields of strangers
on the grace of the seasons
and what the gleaners leave in the corners;
you children of the wind—
birds
that feed on the tree of knowledge
in this place and in every place
to them and to you
a living;

upon Israel
and upon their children and upon all the children of their
    children
in this place and in every place,
to them and to you
life.

# Appendix
# Textual Notes and
# Omitted Poems

In the textual variants minor changes in spelling and punctuation have not been recorded. When variants in a poem or a stanza are many, the entire text has been reprinted for ease of reading. Capitalization in all quotations has been made to conform with Reznikoff's later practice as in the body of this book.

## Contents of Appendix

# I  Notes to *Rhythms* (1918)

## A. Order of Poems

The following tables show how the original ordering of the poems in *Rhythms* was changed in *Poems* (1920) and again in *Five Groups of Verse* (1927). Numbers have been assigned to the unnumbered poems in the first two books. An asterisk indicates a text revised from the printing immediately preceding.

| 1918 | 1920 | 1927 | | 1927 | 1920 | 1918 |
|---|---|---|---|---|---|---|
| 1 | 1* | 1 | | 1 | 1* | 1 |
| 2 | 13* | 10 | | 2 | 2* | 3 |
| 3 | 2* | 2 | | 3* | 6* | 8 |
| 4 | 16* | 16 | | 4 | 5* | 11 |
| 5 | 10* | 15 | | 5* | 7* | 13 |
| | | | | | | |
| 6 | 8 | 17 | | 6* | 15* | 15 |
| 7 | - | - | | 7* | 14* | 14 |
| 8 | 6* | 3* | | 8 | 3 | 17 |
| 9 | - | - | | 9* | 4* | 18 |
| 10 | 9 | 18 | | 10 | 13* | 2 |
| | | | | | | |
| 11 | 5* | 4 | | 11 | 11* | 21 |
| 12 | - | - | | 12* | - | 20 |
| 13 | 7* | 5 | | 13 | 17 | 23 |
| 14 | 14* | 7* | | 14* | 12* | 22 |
| 15 | 15* | 6* | | 15 | 10* | 5 |
| | | | | | | |
| 16 | - | - | | 16 | 16* | 4 |
| 17 | 3 | 8 | | 17 | 8 | 6 |
| 18 | 4* | 9* | | 18 | 9 | 10 |
| 19 | 18* | 19* | | 19* | 18* | 19 |
| 20 | - | 12* | | - | - | 7 |
| | | | | | | |
| 21 | 11* | 11 | | - | - | 9 |
| 22 | 12* | 14* | | - | - | 12 |
| 23 | 17 | 13 | | - | - | 16 |

## B. Textual Variants

1. 1918: The last stanza begins with two lines omitted in 1920 and later: *the wandering body / break into dust;*
2. 1918: First line omitted in 1920 and later: *In this room once belonging to me*
3. 1918: A two-paragraph prose poem, as follows:

    *Think not to shut me up in yourself: I'll drain your beauty, then fling aside the cup.*

So one day tired of the sky and host of stars I'll thrust the
tinsel by.

4. 1918: Title: "The Suicide"
5. 1918: Line 1: line break after spread
6. 1918: Two stanzas, as follows:

They dug her grave so deep
no voice can creep
to her.

She can feel no stir
of joy when her girl sings,
and quietly she sleeps
when her girl weeps.

1920: No stanza breaks.
7. 1918: Text as follows:

The tragedies men move in are mostly played
behind stone walls, shut doors, and curtained windows.
The hero of the fifth act, Death, frequents
dark chambers, rooms with blinds drawn: for he knows
that he is terrible, but only sad
along the highway underneath the sky.
On Brooklyn Bridge I saw a man drop dead.
It meant no more than if he were a sparrow:
for tower on tower behind the bridge arose
the buildings on Manhattan, tall white towers
agleam with lights; below, the wide blue bay
stretched out to meet the high blue sky and the first white star.

1920: As 1927 except line 4: to meet bay and sky.
9. 1918: Line 1: The pale-faced shop-girls leave        No stanza breaks.
1920: As 1927 except no break after line 4.
10. 1918: Text as follows:

Hair and faces glossy with sweat in August
at night through narrow streets glaring with lights
people move as if in funeral processions.
They stand on stoops weeds in a stagnant pool,
they sit at windows waiting for a wind that never comes.
Only the sun, again, like the lidless eye of God.

No one else in the street—but a great wind blowing,
the store-lamps dimmed behind the thickly frosted panes,
the stars like the sun broken and scattered into a million bits.
To-morrow long clouds shutting out the day
and maybe snow or thick rain dropping heavily.

11. 1918: Stanza 2 begins with two lines omitted in 1920 and later: *Among the stones / I came upon his bones:*
12. 1918: Line 3: *white sands;*    Line 4: *And each tree stands a*
    Line 7: *fleet of ships at*
    1920: Poem omitted.
14. 1918: Title: *"On One Whom the Germans Shot"*    Line 1: *are spilled and*    Line 1a: *Gaudier-Brzeska,*
    1920: As 1927 except line 1a retained.
15. 1918: Line 3: *understanding's like*    Line 4: *through a mist*
16. 1918: Title: *"Her Secret Thoughts Were Fingers"*    Subtitle (giving source): *Spoon River Anthology*
19. 1918: Line 1: *My work done, / I sit at the window at ease*    Lines 3-4: *shines / with sunlight. From*
    1920: As 1927 but stanza break between lines 2 and 3.

## C. Omitted Poems

1918: [7]

*Look triumphantly*
*with your face's beauty*
*on others, not on me.*
*I see*
*in your green eyes two leaves*
*of the forbidden tree.*

1918: [9]

*I lost my godhead and became a beast.*
*Circe, you fed him with a feast*
*of kisses. Now, take care, for see*
*what claws have grown on me.*

1918: [12]

*Queen Esther said to herself What is there to fear? We move in our orbits like the stars.*

*But in the night looking at the black fields and river she could not help thinking of Vashti's white cheeks hollowed like shells.*

1918: [16]

*Come away,*
*the clod in the mound*
*will hear no sound*
*and the coffined stone*
*no moan.*
*Come away.*

# II Notes to *Rhythms II* (1919)

## A. Order of Poems

The following tables show how the original ordering of the poems in *Rhythms II* was changed in *Poems* (1920) and again in *Five Groups of Verse* (1927). Numbers have been assigned to the unnumbered poems in the first two books. An asterisk indicates a text revised from the printing immediately preceding.

| 1919 | 1920 | 1927 | | 1927 | 1920 | 1919 |
|---|---|---|---|---|---|---|
| 1 | 2 | 4 | | 1 | 1 | 9 |
| 2 | 5 | 10 | | 2 | 8* | 5 |
| 3 | 6* | 9 | | 3 | 13* | 6 |
| 4 | 9 | 5 [1962*] | | 4 | 2 | 1 |
| 5 | 8* | 2 | | 5 [1962*] | 9 | 4 |
| 6 | 13* | 3 | | 6 | 4 | - |
| 7 | 7* | 15 | | 7 | 11* | 21 |
| 8 | 15 | 14 | | 8 | 10* | 19 |
| 9 | 1 | 1 | | 9 | 6* | 3 |
| 10 | 19 | - | | 10 | 5 | 2 |
| 11 | 17* | 18 | | 11* | 12 | 18 |
| 12 } | 21* | 20* | | 12 | 3 | - |
| 13 } | | | | 13 | 14* | 16 |
| 14 | 20 | - | | 14 | 15 | 8 |
| 15 | 22 | 19 | | 15 | 7* | 7 |
| 16 | 14* | 13 | | 16 | 16* | 22 |
| 17 | 24 | 22 | | 17 | 18* | 23 |
| 18 | 12 | 11* | | 18 | 17* | 11 |
| 19 | 10* | 8 | | 19 | 22 | 15 |
| 20 | 23 | 21 | | 20* | 21* | 12 and 13 |
| 21 | 11* | 7 | | 21 | 23 | 20 |
| 22 | 16* | 16 | | 22 | 24 | 17 |
| 23 | 18* | 17 | | - | 19 | 10 |
| - | 3 | 12 | | - | 20 | 14 |
| - | 4 | 6 | | | | |

## B. Textual Variants

2. 1919: Stanza break after line 2.
3. 1919: Line 1: line break after *knocked*.     No stanza break after line 4.
5. 1919, 1920, 1927: Title: *"In the Ghetto"*
6. 1919: Poem lacking.

7. 1919: Line 3: *rags she cleans*
8. 1919: Text as follows:

   *In the shop she, her mother and grandmother.*

   *Women at windows in still streets*
   *or reading, the glow on their resting hands.*

9. 1919: No stanza break.
11. 1919, 1920: Line 1: *who taught patiently*
12. 1919: Poem lacking.
13. 1919: Title: *"Central Park: Winter"*
15. 1919: Text as follows:

   *Pestilence*

   *Streamers of crepe idling before doors.*

   *Now the huge moon*
   *at the end of the street like a house afire.*

16. 1919: Lines 1-1a: *Mice whisk over the unswept floor, / shadows;*
17. 1919: Lines 2-2a: *toast, / lettuce leaves and a spoonful of mayonnaise.*
    Line 3: *the painted women*
20. 1919: Two poems, as follows:

   [12]

   *She moved effortless,*
   *a swan on a still lake*
   *hardly beating the water with golden feet.*

   *Straight brow and nose,*
   *curved lips and chin.*

   *Sorrow before her*
   *was gone like noise from a street,*
   *snow falling.*

   [13]

   *I remember her all in white*
   *in a house under great trees,*
   *shaded and still in summer;*

   *a white curtain turning in her open window*
   *and a swan dipping a white neck in the trees' shadow.*

   1920: One poem, as follows:

*Like a curtain turning in an open window.*

*Like a swan effortless*
*on a lake shaded and still in summer,*
*dipping a white neck in the trees' shadow,*
*hardly beating the water with golden feet.*

*Sorrow before her*
*was gone like noise from a street,*
*snow falling.*

C. *Omitted Poems*

1919: [10], 1920: [19]

*Delicately rouged,*
*you turn your face*
*and your widened eyes*
*a child seemingly.*

1919: [14], 1920: [20]

*The water broke on the slope of her hips*
*and foamed about her.*
*The slender moon stood in the blue heavens.*

# III  Notes to *Poems* (1920)

## A. Order of Poems

The following tables show how the original ordering of the new work in *Poems* was changed in *Five Groups of Verse* (1927). The poems in the 1920 book have been assigned consecutive numbers; nos. 33-35 appeared under the collective title "Nightmares," and nos. 36-39 under the title "Four of Us." An asterisk indicates a revised text.

| 1920 | 1927 |   | 1927 | 1920 |
|------|------|---|------|------|
| 1 | 1 |  | 1 | 1 |
| 2 | 7 |  | 2* | 3 |
| 3 | 2* |  | 3* | 6 |
| 4 | 14 |  | 4* | 7 |
| 5 | 6* |  | 5* | 8 |
|  |  |  |  |  |
| 6 | 3* |  | 6* | 5 |
| 7 | 4* |  | 7 | 2 |
| 8 | 5* |  | 8 | 29 |
| 9 | 9* |  | 9* | 9 |
| 10 | 24* |  | 10* | 36 |
|  |  |  |  |  |
| 11 | 29 |  | 11*[1962*] | 37 |
| 12} | 23* |  | 12* | 38 |
| 13} |  |  | 13* | 39 |
| 14 | 30* |  | 14 | 4 |
| 15 | 16* |  | 15* | 16 |
|  |  |  |  |  |
| 16 | 15* |  | 16* | 15 |
| 17 | 27* |  | 17 | 25 |
| 18 | - |  | 18 | 27 |
| 19 | - |  | 19 | 28 |
| 20 | 28* |  | 20 | 24 |
|  |  |  |  |  |
| 21 | 21* |  | 21* | 21 |
| 22 | 22* |  | 22* | 22 |
| 23 | - |  | 23* | 12 and 13 |
| 24 | 20 |  | 24* | 10 |
| 25 | 17 |  | 25* | 31 |
|  |  |  |  |  |
| 26 | - |  | 26* | 35 |
| 27 | 18 |  | 27* | 17 |
| 28 | 19 |  | 28* | 20 |
| 29 | 8 |  | 29 | 11 |
| 30 | - |  | 30* | 14 |

| | | | |
|---|---|---|---|
| 31 | 25* | - | 18 |
| 32 | - | - | 19 |
| 33 | - | - | 23 |
| 34 | - | - | 26 |
| 35 | 26* | - | 30 |
| | | | |
| 36 | 10* | - | 32 |
| 37 | 11* | - | 33 |
| 38 | 12* | - | 34 |
| 39 | 13* | | |

## B. Textual Variants

2. 1920: Line 1: *men or boys*     Line 3: *But this*
3. 1920: Two lines as a stanza preceding line 1:

> *Blocking hats with a boy helper*
> *he tells of the sluts he visits.*

Line 1: *Girls outshout*
4. 1920: Line 1: *The fruit pedlar . . . shop loft to shop loft*     Line 2: *on the stone stairs*     Line 3: *and lifting the apple basket on to his knees breathes*
5. 1920: Line 2: *or was it seconds in dozens?*
6. 1920: Line 1: *built dull-red factories*     Line 2: *in the dull-green depths.*
9. 1920: Line 2: *the brown baked apple*     Line 3: *sucks the taste, eating*
10-13. 1920: Printed as a group under the collective title *"Four of Us."*
10. 1920: Text as follows:

### FOUR OF US

#### 1

> *Sleepless, breathing the black air, he heard footsteps along the*
> *      street*
> *and then click, the street-lamp was out,*
> *darkness jumped like a black cat upon his chest.*
>
> *Dawn, the window became grey,*
> *the bed-clothes were lit up and his sleeping wife's head*
> *as if the darkness had gathered and melted into that heap of loose*
> *      hair.*
>
> *Soon her eyes would open, disks of light blue, strange in a Jewess,*
> *he would turn away; for the eyes would look curiously the way*
> *      they had been looking for months,*
> *How are you getting on? Still not doing well?*
> *And her left hand would raise itself slowly and pull on the lobe of*
> *      her left ear;*

and her eyes shine with a slight pity the way a woman looks at a
    mouse in a trap's cage;

no longer the calm look with which she had greeted him
when he was chief clerk at the silk store in the Russian town,
the town he carried about like picture postal-cards in a vest pocket,
edges and colors fast being frayed away.

He had been a clerk thirty years and the firm had grown
and like the moon the chief clerk at his home
shone with the light of the store, the large sun.
Relatives in America would send him money to dole out
to poorer relatives not to be trusted with sums.

Day, the noise of splashing water, somebody washing,
his children in underwear thudding about with bare feet,
pulling on clothes in a hurry and bending over to lace up shoes.
Soon the door would close, again and again, all would be gone,
the three elder to shops, the younger ones to school.

For these he had come to America that they might study and the
    boys be free from army service;
he wanted to lift and spread them as he had been doing, boughs of
    himself the trunk.
Now they were going to work and could study only at night,
snipping bits for years, perhaps ten or more, to make their patched
    learning
and pooling wages to pay for themselves and him and his wife.

He would have liked to gather them into his arms and feed them
    learning
as easily as a baby sucks milk from a woman's breast.
He could only offer to carry them food from the kitchen
or run downstairs to the grocer's for pickles or a bottle of ketchup,
something to make life pleasanter, tastier;
to try to stick hairs in the stiff hide of life and make it a fur to wrap
    them snug.

If only his business were not a flower-pot into which he had spilled
    his money
day by day carefully and now was spilling borrowings,
and nothing came up from the black earth.

His friends had told him that knowing silk and not knowing the
    land's speech,
he should buy a few pieces of silk from a mill-agent or jobber
and job among stores on the East Side.

Thirty years clerk in a store where business was done leisurely,
discussed over glasses of tea in a back-office,
and now to walk the streets and meet men hasty and abrupt.

Without rooms that keep out the waves of wind,
many days toes and fingers sore with cold
between tenements and barrels heaped with ashes or garbage.

Once he had gone beyond the known streets,
no Jewish signs nor were the houses as tall,
another poverty drizzled upon them.
Three young men were loafing in front of an empty store.
They smiled as he passed. Something pasty struck his cheek.
He looked at what had fallen off wet and blackened by gutter-
    water.
He looked back at the laughing three, one was ready to throw
    something else.

He would never do well. The stores bought directly from places he
    bought at and as cheaply,
those who had no credit with others he could not trust.
He had made sales to stores whose owner's credit
was not bad but not above worry, sales at a trifling profit,
perhaps more than average, but he would have to sell much more
    than he did.

Younger relatives now excused themselves after a few words
and hurried into the noise of their shops to some matter of their
    own.
Men who sold him goods were vexed at his small purchases.

The day was the first warm day of spring.
The sunlight fell in large living oblongs on the wooden floor;
he opened a window, the air blew in warm and fragrant
as if a gardener were mowing grass below.

But this sunlight showed where his shoes' leather had cracked and
    gaped,
his faded trousers, the bottoms frayed with walking,
showed his clothes like a symbol of himself.

He had no money. Borrow again?
Not from his kin and his children had such need of theirs.

In winter when rain drummed on stone and glass marches at night
    and sullen war
or when the streets were heaped with snow turning black
his own music was sung and his own despair imaged.

But now in spring he was forgotten easily like the thought of
    somebody else's sorrow.
The flagged yards and the fire-escapes were glinting with sunlight
and the tall fences dirtied by rain with their rows of nails on top,
    bleeding rust.

*Women were opening windows and shaking clothes joyously into*
    *the yards,*
*his own wife had gone to the grocer or butcher, his children were*
    *at work or school,*
*only he was useless like an old pot left in the kitchen for a while.*

*He pulled down the window-shade and laid himself near the stove.*
*He liked the floor's hardness.*
*The pour of gas sickened him, he was half-minded to pull the*
    *rubber tube out of his mouth,*
*but he felt weak and dizzy, too weak to move his hand.*

11. 1920: Line 1: *by the top-floor window*      Line 2: *and looked over the tenement into the sky*      Line 3: *where the new moon was like a girl alone on a roof thinking.*      Line 5: *tears at the sore within her*      Line 6: *smile, her eyes clear.*      Line 7: stanza break precedes      Line 7a: *She who once slim and gentle would soon be clumsy, talking harshly.*      Line 8: printed as a separate stanza.
1927: As 1962 but retains the extra stanza of lines 7 and 7A.
Line 7a: *she who, slim and gentle once, would soon become clumsy, talking harshly.*
12. 1920: Line 1: *pitch-dark. The gas had been turned off by the company.* Stanza break follows.      Line 1a: *A candle-light before him, hot wax dripping over his fingers,*      Line 2: *his old room*
Line 2a: *his sister removing the furniture had emptied desk and bookcase in a heap.*      Line 3: *through books and papers.*
Line 7: *ought to have known the*      Line 9: *died down.*
Line 10: *the white paper into*      Line 11a: *There was no need to read them first, he knew the contents word by word.*      Line 14: *for an instant before*      Line 15: *sick with its one window opening on the parlour.*      Line 16a: *He walked into his den again. The white box?*      Line 17: *gauze. Moths flew out like dust.*
13. 1920: Line 1: *From her bed she . . . the snow-flakes crossing*
Line 9a: *over the plains*      Line 10: *between fields*
15. 1920: Line 1: *The slender tree stands alone*      Line 2: two lines, as follows: *between the roofs of the far town / and the wood far away like a low hill.*      Line 3: *In the vast open*
16. 1920: No title. Text as follows:

*The city breaks in houses to the sea, uneasy with waves,*
*and the lonely sun clashes like brass cymbals.*
*In the streets truck-horses, muscles sliding under the steaming hides,*
*pound the sparks flying about their hoofs;*
*and fires, those gorgeous beasts, squirm in the furnaces*
*under the looms weaving us.*

*At evening by cellars cold with air of rivers at night,*
*we, whose lives are only a few words,*
*watch the young moon leaning over the baby at her breast*
*and the stars small to our littleness.*

21. 1920: Line 1: *again low words*      Lines 2a and 2b: an additional stanza:

> *The rays of the orderly street-lamps, drops of light in the darkness,*
> *keep pointing to us.*

22. 1920: Line 2a: *and sat around, dark spaces about a sun.*     Line 5: *Within and about*
23. 1920: Two separate poems, as follows:

### [12]

> *Hour after hour in easy-chairs on the porch rocking,*
> *hearing the wind in shade trees along the street*
> *and looking into the yard's green growth.*
>
> *At times a storm comes up and the dust is blown in long curves*
>     *along the street,*
> *over the carts driven slowly, drivers and horses nodding.*
>
> *Afterwards the still clouds; children too young to be at school*
>     *come out to play*
> *with little shrill voices.*
>
> *Thoughts are taken up and put aside, nothing cut into, nothing is*
>     *done,*
> *but pleasant meetings of friend with friend, short walks,*
> *daily food and the long sleep at nights.*

### [13]

> *Years are thrown away as if I were immortal,*
> *by day selling and looking pleasant*
> *and the nights spent in talking*
> *shining words, sometimes, like fireflies in the darkness,*
> *lighting and going out and after all no light.*
>
> *I think at times of some of the plans I had.*

24. 1920: Line 1: *street with head*
25. 1920: No title and an additional line, as follows:

> *Trees shrugging their shoulders in the wind*
> *and the ceaseless weaving of the uneven water.*

26. 1920: No title but printed as the third of three poems under the collective title *"Nightmares."* (For the other two see the "Omitted Poems" that follow.) Text as follows:

> *The street is white and cold under the huge moon,*
> *the trees' shadows lie in black pools on the lawns.*

27.  1920: No title. Text as follows:

> Trees standing far off in winter
> against a polished blue sky
> with boughs blown about like brown hair;
>
> the stiff lines of the twigs
> blurred by April buds;
>
> or branches crowded with leaves
> and a wind turning
> their dark green light.

28.  1920: Line 1: *moon's rim and*
30.  1920: Order of stanzas reversed.

## C. Omitted Poems

### 1920: [18]

> On the shaken water
> of the shining sea
> we lay like seaweed
> carelessly.
>
> Afterwards running
> with outstretched hands
> we chase each other
> across the sands.

### 1920: [19]

> I look at her through spectacles
> and remember women
> whom I saw for a while
> walking on and away.

### 1920: [23]

> Steam-shovel, in the hollow where yard and poplars were,
> going home we would look at the rows of poplars.

### 1920: [26]

> She woke at a child crying
> and turned to the empty cradle,
> forgetting.

### 1920: [30]

> Under the heavens furrowed with clouds
> a man behind his stumbling plough.

1920: [32]

The rain fell and stopped but the clouds stayed
over the warehouses lonely at night.

1920: [33] and [34]

## NIGHTMARES

### I

The elevated railroad made the street darker than others
and it had no stores.

Walking there after midnight I saw an old man coming.

We passed and I walked a long way and suddenly turned,
he stood where I had left him, looking after me.

I turned a corner and hid in a doorway, waiting to see if he would follow.
I waited long and then I saw his deformed shadow coming slowly.

I felt for the door-knob. The door was locked.
I bit my clenched fingers to keep from screaming.

### II

Up a street that a railway overhead made a tunnel
he pushed through the shuffling men to a lame beggar with a girl of twelve
and hit the beggar's back. The girl stared, the men shuffled by.

The beggar and the girl hurried on; with a long step, laughing, he was up to
    them
and kept hitting the turning beggar.

Her hair fell over the girl's face and she stuck her chin out trying to drag the
    beggar away
and the beggar kept raising his hands, head turning, twisting feet and body
    along
in a knot which is being unravelled,
questioning the face of the laughing man
and the incurious faces of the men shuffling by.

Seeing an ice-cream cart he called the girl away from the beggar.
She gorged on a bar of frozen rainbow
and he placed the pennies on the wet top of the cart, laughing.

## IV Notes to *Uriel Accosta: A Play* and *A Fourth Group of Verse* (1921)

### A. Order of Poems

The following tables show how the order of the poems in *Uriel Accosta* was changed in *Five Groups of Verse* (1927). The last twenty-seven poems in 1921 were numbered under the collective title "Jews"; the poems preceding that group were unnumbered. Here all the poems have been assigned consecutive numbers. An asterisk indicates a revised text.

| 1921 | 1927 | | 1927 | 1921 |
|------|------|---|------|------|
| 1 | 19* | | 1* | 4 |
| 2 | 40* | | 2* | 5 |
| 3 | 47* | | 3* | 6 |
| 4 | 1* | | 4* | 9 |
| 5 | 2* | | 5* | 10 |
| | | | | |
| 6 | 3* | | 6 | 12 |
| 7 | - | | 7* | 8 |
| 8 | 7* | | 8 | 16 |
| 9 | 4* | | 9* | 15 |
| 10 | 5* | | 10* | 19 |
| | | | | |
| 11 | - | | 11* | 13 and 14 |
| 12 | 6 | | 12* | 17 |
| 13⎫ | | | 13* | 18 |
| 14⎭ | 11* | | 14* | 20 |
| 15 | 9* | | 15* | 21 |
| | | | | |
| 16 | 8 | | 16* | 23 |
| 17 | 12* | | 17* | 22 |
| 18 | 13* | | 18* | 24 |
| 19 | 10* | | 19* | 1 |
| 20 | 14* | | 20* | 25 |
| | | | | |
| 21 | 15* | | 21* | 26 |
| 22 | 17* | | 22* | 27 |
| 23 | 16* | | 23* | 28 |
| 24 | 18* | | 25* | 29 |
| 25 | 20* | | 25* | 30 |
| | | | | |
| 26 | 21* | | 26* | 31 |
| 27 | 22* | | 27* | 32 |
| 28 | 23* | | 28* | 33 |
| 29 | 24* | | 29* | 34 |
| 30 | 25* | | 30* | 35 |

| | | | |
|---|---|---|---|
| 31 | 26* | 31* | 36 |
| 32 | 27* | 32* | 37 |
| 33 | 28* | 33* | 38 |
| 34 | 29* | 34* | 39 |
| 35 | 30* | 35* | 40 |
| | | | |
| 36 | 31* | 36* | 41 |
| 37 | 32* | 37* | 42 |
| 38 | 33* | 38 | 43 |
| 39 | 34* | 39* | 44 |
| 40 | 35* | 40* | 2 |
| | | | |
| 41 | 36* | 41* | 45 |
| 42 | 37* | 42* | 46 |
| 43 | 38 | 43* | 47 |
| 44 | 39* | 44* | 48 |
| 45 | 41* | 45* | 49 |
| | | | |
| 46 | 42* | 46* | 50 |
| 47 | 43* | 47* | 3 |
| 48 | 44* | 48* | 51 |
| 49 | 45* | - | 7 |
| 50 | 46* | - | 11 |
| | | | |
| 51 | 48* | | |

## B. Textual Variants

1. 1921: Title: *"Sunday Walks"*          Line 1: *Over stones*          line break after *dust*; remainder printed as new line.          Line 2: printed as two lines with break after *gloom,*          Line 3: *slime. Beyond, thickets of*          Line 4: *tree stretched up, dead.*          Line 5: *A dead duck lay, head*          Line 6: *tide was out . . . pool lay on the*          Line 7: *Someone had thrown*          Line 8: *of tin cans rusted;*          Line 9: *rust, crept in*          Line 10: *clouds showed like*

2. 1921: Line 3: *as finger knuckles, seated upon the*          Line 9: *away so many*

3. 1921: No title. Line 4: *fish mouldy*

4. 1921: Line 1: *Under grey cloud*          Line 3: *their shadows of smoke*

5. 1921: No title. Line 1: *Between factory chimneys grease*          Line 2: *In the drizzle tugs drag their guts of smoke.*

7. 1921: Line 8: *white tops of*          Line 9: *into whiffs of spray*          Line 17: *were towns*          Line 23: *flew in the wind over the lake.*

9. 1921: Before line 1 a deleted line: *In the restaurant panelled with mirrors, the old woman faces her daughter.*

10. 1921: Line 1: *and the knights*          Line 2: line break after *open,*          Line 2a: *pulling their guts*

11(I). 1921: Line 1: *night." "Good night." Another day gone.*          Line 4: *about? Then supper and chat, chat.*

11(II). 1921: Line 2: *Why am I taking trouble to please him? I talk. I turn*

12. 1921: Line 1: *than wind*
13. 1921: Line 1: *In spring sparrows* Stanza break after line 1.
14. 1921: Line 1: *trees stand in*
15. 1921: Line 2: *Here on the . . . girl rakes the fallen leaves*
16. 1921: Deleted first line: *Do you remember that summer when we were in the country* Line 1: *and we* Line 2: *beyond?*
    Line 3: printed as continuation of line 2. Line 5: *yellow daisies and golden-rod* Line 6a: *and we walked about in the blaze over our heads and hands.*
17. 1921: Line 1: *dinner on Sunday afternoon we* Line 2: *into the . . . the marsh along the bay* Line 3: *blue cloudless sky* Line 4: *would watch the base-ball players; in the noisy,*
    Line 5: *Afterwards, in the evening, glad and at ease, we walked back to the city, stretching out rows* Line 6: *lamp after lamp lighting as the . . . way, or women*
18. 1921: Line 1: *I woke. Swiftly* Line 4: *Hidden from me in*
19. 1921: Text as follows:

> He showed me the album. "But this?" I asked.
> I knew his sister, her face somewhat the picture's but none of that
>     delicacy.
> "My mother before her marriage." Coming in, I had met
> a round-shouldered woman with a shrivelled face.
> His father at the table with friends still out-shouted the wheels,
> though the day's work was done and the shop closed until morning.
> Afterwards I left and went through their candy store with one
>     show-case of candy,
> in little heaps in little saucers, ever so many for a penny.
> A single gas-jet flared in the empty store. They kept no lights in the
>     window. I stepped into the night.

20-48. Twenty-seven of the twenty-nine poems that follow were numbered and printed in 1921 under the collective title, *"Jews."* The exceptions are numbers 40 and 47 below.
20. 1921: Line 1: *before supper.* Line 2: *the curtains.* Line 3: *It had been snowing, the street under the black sky was bluish white.* Line 6: combined with line 5 as *The boys were after him.*
    Line 7a: *The room was cold. They put ashes on the fire before going to bed.* Line 11: *He stopped, standing knee-deep* Line 14: *snow. Houses and streets were still.*
21. 1921: The following stanza precedes line 1:

> His grandfather was a wisp of a man with a little beard.
> He led grandfather home through Seventh Street Park.
> A knot of men were larking with a girl. They pushed a man into
>     grandfather.
> He fell and rolled, covered with dust, to the railing.

Line 2: *Only on holy days he went out of the house to synagogue.*
Line 4: *happened, only on* No stanza break between lines 5 and 6. Line 6: *Kippur his uncle* Line 6a: *And the boy*

*stayed home, relieved.*     Stanza break between lines 6a and 7.

22. 1921: Lines 3 and 4: printed as one line.     Lines 9 and 10: printed as one line.     Line 11: *In March*     Line 13: *large and color*     Line 16: *tree was still and the branches, only the end twigs moved a little.*     Line 17: *thought, "Trees are symmetrical —and whatever grows and lives—in shape—and in change during the years.*     Line 17a: *So my own life is symmetrical and the lives of men."*     Lines 18 and 19: printed as one line.

23. 1921: Line 3: *Under bushes*     Line 4: *lakes and air,* Lines 3 and 4 printed as one line.     Line 5: *on the earth.* Line 6: *and there spread, and there holes, globules hanging in disorder. He thought, "The symmetry in growth and life on earth, our sense of order,*     Line 7: *Is uncontrolling in the universe of these wheels."*

24. 1921: Line 1: *and children to make a home.*     Line 3: *teach him for an hour, night after night.*     Stanza break after line 3: Lines 6 and 7 printed as one line.     Stanza break after line 8. Line 12: *High school would*     Stanza break after line 17. Line 19: *throat, with his*     Line 21: *back the chair*     Stanza break after line 22.     Line 22a: *She came back late. She asked the women on the stoop if her mother was home.*     Line 22b: *Where have you been?" "In the library, Ma." She told her mother nothing.*

25. 1921: Line 1: *From where he lay in the sun the trees*     Line 2: *a dull white*     Lines 6 and 7 printed as one line.     Line 7a: *She came, almost skipping, over the turf; and went her way and was gone.*

26. 1921: Lines 6ff: two stanzas, as follows:

> *He might go to her house at last. They were all up, preparing*
> *    breakfast.*
> *The smell of coffee filled the screened porch.*
> *Her glance bid him welcome. She always spoke little and then low.*
> *Such restraint was in her speech*
> *and in the curving of her body and hands*
> *as she went about her tasks.*
>
> *The sunlight edged a way upon the porch*
> *and when she walked through it, her yellow hair and the white*
> *    flesh of her hands shone.*

27. 1921: Line 2: *his paper sliced . . . table in back.*     Stanza breaks after lines 2, 5, and 7.     Line 9: *knew she*

28. 1921: Line 1: *mother, almost a dwarf, stepped*     Line 2: *stopped to a*     Stanza break after line 2.     Line 4: *houses were set* Line 5: *take skates*     Line 10: *Webber's coat. Webber* Stanza break after line 10.     Line 18: *ask fellas about* Stanza break after line 18.     Line 25: line break after test? Remainder combined with line 26.     Stanza break after line 28.     Line 31: *go walking.*

29. 1921: Line 1: *closing, windows*     Line 2: *At last, only a light left here and there of other book-keepers still working.*     Lines 3a, 3b, and 3c:

*He could see his father seating himself upon the window-sill and*
*jumping off.*
*They found his body on the flags of the yard behind the tenement*
*in which they lived.*
*Since he had been unable to find work and keep at least himself,*
*his note read, he did not want to be a burden to his wife and son.*

Stanza break after line 3c.　　　Line 4: *He had worked enough for*
*that night. He went*　　　Line 5: *about a chasm. Suppose he*
Line 6: *Who was to . . . down, head first?*　　　Lines 6a and 6b:

*But the shop windows had been left open. He slowly went to the*
*first window with his back toward it.*
*He must think just of going downstairs and not think beyond the*
*bannister.*

30. Line 1: *She entered high school and found charm in Latin and*
Line 5: *student in one*　　　Line 6: *reading evenings, but*
Line 7: *books he knew* Line break after *living.* Remainder combined
with line 8.　　　Line 8: *you'll be old*　　　Line 9a: *When her*
*daughter was born, she began to plan for her education.*
31. 1921: Line 1: *The boy next . . . and sit listening*　　　Line 3:
*evening she spoke*　　　Line 7: *father would speak kindly*
Line 8: *began asking for*　　　Line 11: *taken this notion*
Line 13: *When they were out walking, Gabriel*　　　Line 17: *saved*
*fifty dollars from*　　　Line 18: *cotton jobbers and*　　　Line 20:
*as if blown up.*　　　Line 22: *reached his father's home*
32. 1921: Lines 1 and 1a:

*He came home late that night and was afraid to go through the*
*grocery store,*
*where his father was still talking to customers. He went through*
*the tenement hallway into the room, back of the store, where*
*they ate and slept.*

Line 3: *stood looking up at him*　　　Line 6: *basement store. It*
　　　Line 9: *around to neighbors.*　　　Lines 11 and 12: printed
as one line: *"Well." "But I hear from relatives you're trying to borrow*
*money?" "Yes." His father paused. "I hope you get it."*
33. 1921: Line 1: *He remembered how passing the shop after high school,*
*he had looked up at the sign and gone on, glad*　　　Line 2: *saw his*
*parents' hair grey and heard*　　　Line 5: *into; but I have always let*
*you have your own way."*　　　No stanza break after line 5.
Line 6: *went selling . . . read* Arrival
34. 1921: Line 2: *through public school*　　　Line 3: *father engaged her*
*to his . . . face, was short and a little fat.*　　　Line 4: *hates me, he*
*hates me!"*　　　Line 4a: *The marriage was elaborate. Her father*
*was well-to-do and she was the only daughter.*　　　Line 5: *bought*
*her husband a*　　　Lines 5 and 6: printed as one line: *bought her*
*husband a . . . had saved up money.*　　　Line 7: *buy at once, he*
　　　Line 8: *men's smell when . . . ditching. He cheated*

Line 10: *refused him money. He came home.*     Line 11: *The two older*

35. 1921: Line 1: *came to his . . . clouds bunk together."*     Line 2: *He recited at parties when he was older well-known rants. They* Line 3: *he made the acquaintance of . . . lawyer. There were rumors of partnerships.*     Line 6: *work, behind a counter, among* Line 8: *but now he*     Line 9: line break after *making.*

36. 1921: Line 1: *Walking was too slow, he ran softly on the balls of his feet. In a*     Stanza break after line 2.     Line 3: *was sitting up*     Stanza break after line 4.     Line 5: *He sat moodily. He thought*     Line 6: *He thought of noting*     Line 7: *her eyes to-night.*

37. 1921: Line 1: printed as two lines: *man / and on*     Line 3: *Once she saw his mouth jerk, and*     Line 5: *but said nothing.* Line 7: *awake at night*     Line 8: *Next morning she went down to his store but it*     Line 9: printed as two lines: *searched. / For* Line 10: *prosperous and he had left it, bank . . . all, untouched.*     Line 12: printed as two lines: *city. / One* Line 13: printed as two lines: *children. / She*

39. 1921: Line 5: first sentence printed with line 4: *not help laughing. / Sure*     Line 6: *he roomed and boarded in the home of a . . . had kept herself through high school, giving lessons, and was now in* Line 8: *arm to cure. He sat silently*     Stanza deleted, lines 9a, 9b, and 9c:

    The doctor warned him not to go back to work as a smith.
    He tried to learn how to make wire-frames in a cousin's shop,
    but his fingers were stiff.

    Line 11-12: line break after *discovered him / and searched for . . . cores in the gutter to throw . . . they walked past, as if intent*     Lines 13a and 13b:

    Finally, he would just walk through the street once or twice of an
      evening. Once he thought he saw her. His heart bounded as if
      struck.
    He stood still to steady himself; but the girl, coming nearer, he saw
      it was not she.

40. 1921: Line 1: *mother came and sat beside him. "What are you reading? Read*     Line 2: *"But you . . . Ma. What's the use?" "Read me a little. What do you care?"*     Line 6: *He read to her and she listened*     Line 7: *sheets she*     Line 8: *And from*

41. 1921: Line 3: *had been scrimping from day to day all*     Line 4: *When his uncle died, he left*     Line 6: *but within a year he*

42. 1921: Line 3: *near the railroad tracks and the*     Stanza break after line 3.     Line 4: *father had been sick for years; but he was . . . merchandise."*     Line 5: *of. He gave up his studies and taught in a school on the East Side.*     Line 6: *three, and others . . . most came*     Line 8: *and evening, daily; Sunday he slept all morning and afterwards took a walk.*     No stanza break after

line 8.          Line 10: *forty. It had been book and books when a boy,*
*he had to win prizes and a scholarship to keep going. And now so many*
*years in the school.*          Line 11: *whom he would care to*
Line 12: *up his work to what else . . . turn? He felt afraid to break the*
*routine which he had grown used to.*

43. 1921: Line 3: *There's a Chinese restaurant upstairs. Water came*
*through the ceiling and damaged silk. The water*          Line 4:
*kinds of engineers; they*

44. 1921: Text as follows:

> Her daughters were well married; their husbands earned enough
>     and more each year. Both could afford maids; she always
>     found their children clean and happy.
> Her husband's business was good and they had as much as two
>     elderly people needed. They went to theatre oftener than they
>     used to. She was planning to buy new furniture.
>
> Her younger daughter died in childbirth. Her son-in-law married
>     again. Coming to see the children, she could not help crying
>     for her dead daughter.
> Her son-in-law had to ask her not to call.
>
> Now when she woke it was broad day. Her husband had gone to
>     the store long before.
> She wrapped her head and shoulders in a shawl, knitting her
>     thoughts.
> She got up at last and poured herself some brandy. The room was
>     cold.
> When she went out she took a brandy flask in her bag to nip in
>     lavatories.
> Her older daughter's husband forbade her the house. She was noisy
>     about her dead daughter when drunk. And there were the
>     children and the neighbors.
>
> Her older daughter died in childbirth.
> Her son-in-law married again. The new wife took the older children
>     from school and sent them to work.
> They became coarse, their house was full of quarrelling.
>
> Their grandmother was now in an asylum. Her husband came to
>     see her. Once he saw the lunatic children playing in the yard.
> "Why do you cry?" she asked. He pointed. "You cry for them but
>     not for me."
> Afterwards she told her husband, "I am sharpening a knife to kill
>     my grandchildren; but not you, you must pay for my board
>     here."

45. 1921: Line 2: *Once the stores were burned*          Line 4: *sign on his*
          Line 7: *do with Mendel?" . . . Siberia." "Do you think it*
*would be right for me to place a Jew*          Line 9: *grandchildren*
*took them into the streets to sell.*          Lines 10 and 11: printed as
one line: *money. His son, the*

46.  1921: Text as follows:

> His daughter belonged to a club. The club studied modern literature
> and met, once a month, in each other's house.
> When his daughter's turn came she told him that the club would
> come. That evening they were to discuss Maeterlinck; but the
> old man thought that they were coming to meet him.
> They were seated at last in the parlor. Embarrassed, she asked them
> not to begin; her father wanted to speak to them.
> The members whispered to each other, "Who is her father?"
> "I thank you, young men and women," he said, "for the honor of
> your visit. I suppose you would like to hear me recite some of
> my poems." He began to chant.

47.  1921: No title. Line 1: *The neighbors*      Line 2: *because her figure was*      Line 2a: *and, it was said, her husband had been a shoemaker before becoming a doctor.*      Line 4: *newcomers*
Line 5: *afterwards, and these to others, and*      Line 10: *conductor came and raised*      Line 15: *became so hot*      Line 16: *station. The*      Line 18: *drink, ah good! If*

48.  1921: Line 1: *beside the bench*      Line 3: *begin. Though it was early the sunny . . . walked near the houses.*      Line 4: *finish and then he*      Stanza break after line 4.      Line 5: *with a black*      Stanza break after line 6.      Line 9: *work at the*

## C. Omitted Poems

### 1921: [7]

#### Office Help

*Morning after morning the sun shone.*

*She kept making her entries*
*until the street*
*filled with twilight.*

### 1921: [11]

*In the even curves of gutters and even curves of gutters*
*the irregular slope of the park's barren hill.*

## V   Note to *Five Groups of Verse* (1927)

Textual Variant

20.   1927: between stanzas 2 and 3 the following stanza omitted in 1962:

> *The altar blazes. I bring*
> *my thoughts to heap upon it.*
> *The smoke of my breath*
> *is an offering.*

# VII   Notes to *Jerusalem the Golden* (1934)

Textual Variants

3.  1934: Line 8: *look longingly at moon*
8.  1934: Poem opens with the following stanza:

> *This morning the dawn*
> *did not redden the white wooden frame of the window;*
> *the rain drops hang in a row*
> *from the rail of the fire-escape.*

22.  1934: Poem ends with following three lines:

> *In front of the pigeon house the white pigeons*
> *are preening themselves; in the yard*
> *white chickens with bright red combs bustle about.*

28.  1934: Title: *"Idyll"*
46.  1934: Poem opens with the following stanza:

> *The squads, platoons, and regiments*
> *of lighted windows,*
> *ephemeral under the evening star—*

Line 1: *feast*
70.  1934: Poem opens with the following stanza:

> *The green water of the lake brimming over*
> *in silence,*
> *quietly in motion.*

# VIII   Notes to *In Memoriam: 1933* (1934)

Textual Variants

7. 1934: 2nd paragraph, line 7: *leaders of the phalanx, of legions*
   Line 8: *masters of chariots, of the long*

# IX  Notes to *Separate Way* (1936)

**Textual Variants**

1. 1934: part IV, line 1: *How pleasant is the wind, or the sun.*
   Line 1a: *to those behind windows;*          Line 2: *and the silence*
2. 1934: Title: *"Malicious Women Greet You"*
3. 1934: Title: *"Insignificance"*          Part II not reprinted in 1962.
8. Stanzas 4 and 5 not reprinted in 1962.

# Index of Titles
and First Lines

Entries in italics refer to texts in the Appendix.

221

*Photo: Gerard Malanga*

Charles Reznikoff was born in a Jewish ghetto in Brooklyn in 1894. His parents were immigrants from Russia. He was graduated from the Brooklyn Boys' High School when not quite sixteen, spent a year at the new School of Journalism of the University of Missouri (1910-1911), and entered the law school of New York University in 1912. Admitted to the bar of the State of New York in 1916, he practiced only briefly. The United States had entered the First World War and in 1918 he was admitted to the officers' training camp at Columbia University, but before he received any training the war was over. His parents were then in business as manufacturers of hats and, for a while, he was a salesman for them, selling to jobbers and large department stores. In 1928, he went to work writing law for the firm publishing *Corpus Juris*, an encyclopedia of law for lawyers. Later, he worked in Hollywood for about three years for a friend who was then a producer for Paramount Pictures. After that, he made his living by freelance writing, research, translating, and editing. In 1962, New Directions published a selection of his verse, *By the Waters of Manhattan*. He was awarded the Jewish Book Council of America's award for English poetry in 1963 and in 1971 the Morton Dauwen Zabel Award for Poetry by the National Institute of Arts and Letters.

He was married in 1930 to Marie Syrkin, now Professor Emeritus of Humanities, Brandeis University.

The present book is the first volume of Reznikoff's *Complete Poems*, edited by Seamus Cooney.

As this book was in press, word came of the death of Charles Reznikoff in New York on January 22, 1976.